Graphic Content

Graphic Content

True Stories From Top Creatives

PRINT

Cincinnati, Ohio

Curated by Brian Singer

For more excellent books and resources for designers, visit www.howdesign.com.

17 16 15 14   5 4 3 2 1

ISBN-13: 978-1-4403-3327-9

Distributed in Canada by Fraser Direct
100 Armstrong Avenue
Georgetown, Ontario, Canada L7G 5S4
Tel: (905) 877-4411

Distributed in the U.K. and Europe by F&W Media International, LTD
Brunel House, Forde Close, Newton Abbot, TQ12 4PU, UK
Tel: (+44) 1626 323200, Fax: (+44) 1626 323319
Email: enquiries@fwmedia.com

Distributed in Australia by Capricorn Link
P.O. Box 704, Windsor, NSW 2756 Australia
Tel: (02) 4560-1600

Design: Brian Singer (www.iamsomeguy.com)
Art Director: Claudean Wheeler
Editor: Scott Francis
Production Coordinator: Greg Nock

Typefaces:
Harriet, designed by Jackson Cavanaugh, Okay Type.
Akzidenz-Grotesk, designed by Günter Gerhard Lange, H. Berthold AG.

Brian Singer is a San Francisco based artist and designer. He works at Facebook, where he leads a team of designers, engineers and filmmakers.

Brian is the creator of The 1000 Journals Project, a global art experiment that has been covered in the *New York Times, San Francisco Chronicle, Wall Street Journal*, and many others. It is the subject of a book, a documentary, and was exhibited at both the San Francisco Museum of Modern Art and the Skirball Cultural Center in Los Angeles.

When no one is looking, Brian creates intricate and provocative art projects under his alter ego "Someguy" (iamsomeguy.com).

In 2013, Brian joined the national board of AIGA, the professional association for design. Prior to that, he was president of the San Francisco Chapter of AIGA and served on the advisory board for the San Francisco Arts Commission Gallery.

Thank you. Thank you. Thank you.

While the final book might look nice and orderly, the process getting here wasn't. I want to thank Eric Baker for planting the seed for this book with his amazing stories, Chris, Heidi and the HILL crew for putting on the Creative Summit and providing inspiration for designers, young as well as "seasoned", Kevin Toyama for his help and guidance along the way, and Scott Francis and Claudean Wheeler from Print Books for keeping this project from derailing (despite my best efforts). Finally, this book couldn't exist without all the generous contributors. Thank you to everyone who shared their stories. This is your book.

Table of Contents

> What the world
> needs now is
> another book
> about design.

Introduction: a long story short

We're sipping Scotch on the porch of the Country Inn & Suites in San Marcos, Texas. It's the final night of the Creative Summit and Eric Baker breaks into a story about his favorite grade school teacher and reuniting with her after many, many years. We're captivated as he speaks, and I'm touched deeply by his story. As I sit in wonderment at how amazing life is, it strikes me that these kinds of stories, the ones we share over drinks or at dinner parties, are often the most meaningful.

Now, I doubt that anyone has ever sat back and thought to themselves "What the world needs now is another book about design." (Actually, I suspect quite a few people think that.) But what about a different type of book? Something more than career advice for young designers (be true to yourself, follow your dreams, blah blah blah).

You have stories. The time you got arrested in Rio and had to bribe your way out of jail, or the time you took your 101-year-old grandmother skydiving. There was the night you met Robert Downey Jr. in the Men's restroom, and the prank you played on your high school principal. These are the experiences from your life that you share with friends to amaze, surprise, and entertain them.

So here we are. What follows is a collection of true stories, as shared by a variety of creative types who graciously agreed to contribute. Some may shock you or make you laugh, while others will stir up deep emotions. At least one will bore you (we all have that *one* friend; you know who I'm talking about). So grab a glass of Scotch, put your feet up, and let's start at the beginning.

— Brian Singer

Mrs. Allen

by Eric Baker

It was 1959, San Diego and I was just a weird ten-year-old kid, who wanted to be a Beatnik. This was the during Eisenhower years. Conformity was the rule of the day.

At the start of fourth grade, I was praying I would get Mrs. Allen as my teacher. She was young (maybe twenty-eight) and very beautiful and funny. The gods shined on me, and I got the best teacher I ever had.

Naturally I was madly in love with Mrs. Allen. At the start of the year she gave the class reading aptitude tests. I scored high and she began to bring me books to read: Jack London, Mark Twain, Hemingway. I gobbled them up—partly, I think, just to impress her—and books became a huge part of my life.

I was a troublemaker and jokester, always disrupting things. Once while reading to the class I was talking (naturally) and she told me to be quiet. Ten minutes later, same thing. She said "Don't do it again." I did and she threw the book and hit me right in the back off the head. You could do that then. I deserved it!

At the end of the school year she was expecting her first child and my mother knitted a pink and blue baby blanket for the baby. She came back to school to visit with her new baby girl, but I never saw Mrs. Allen again after that.

As I got older I would think of her often and wondered about her life. I tried everything to find her; called the school, the board of education, Google, Yellow pages ... nothing.

Several years ago I was at my neighbor's house having coffee and I told him the story. He's a big-deal reporter at *The New York Times*. He was at his computer and asked me her name: "Yvonne Allen." "Southern California?" "Yeah" I said. "Here is her phone number and address."

I called right away, got voicemail but did not leave a message, after about the fourth call a woman answered the phone. I asked "Is this Yvonne Allen?" The woman said, "No, this is her daughter."

I said "I know this is a long shot but was your mother a teacher in the 1950s in San Diego?"

"Yes," she said.

"Oh, Thank God" I said. "She was my all-time favorite teacher and I just loved her."

Hesitantly the woman asked, "Did my mother ever throw a book at you?"

"Yes," I said, "and I deserved it!"

"You're Eric Baker," she said. "You were famous in our family. You were my mom's favorite student, and I was the baby your mother made the blanket for. It was my favorite blanket".

Amazing. I asked if her mom was there and she said no, she was in the hospital. I said, "I hope nothing serious." She replied, "Yes, actually she has terminal cancer and not a lot of time." I was so sad. The daughter, Leslie, said that her mom would be home in a few days and to call back.

A few days later I called and Leslie answered the phone. She was excited I had called. "Mom," she said, "I think you'll want to take this call."

"Hello?"

"Mrs. Allen, this is Eric Baker. It's been a long time, but I hope you'll remember me."

Shrieking laughter. "Oh, Eric, it is so good to hear from you."

We talked for over an hour, laughed and cried. I told her how madly in love with her I was. She laughed and said she knew. I told her how the love of books she had instilled in me was a huge part of my life and that I actually earned a living designing books and other things. It was just a wonderful, poignant experience.

I sent her some of the books I had designed and spoke with her the day after she received them. I had designed a book by Baudelaire called *Invitation to the Voyage*. It was a love poem. She said it was her favorite. I told her it was the one book I was most proud of.

A few days later I called and Leslie answered. I asked after her mother and she said, "Eric, I'm sorry, but Mom died yesterday." I knew it was coming and while I was sad, I was also happy that, at the end, we were able to connect.

Before she died I said, "Mrs. Allen, since I am almost sixty, can I call you Yvonne?" She laughed and said, "Of course you can, Eric. You're an old friend."

Leslie told me how happy she was that we had reunited after so many years. It was a wonderful thing that had happened. I was lucky; Mrs. Allen was the best.

Eric Baker is an independent designer specializing in branding and identity systems for a number of hospitality, publishing, retail, entertainment and cultural concerns.

Along with branding he produces a wide range of work in the fields of hospitality, publishing and corporate communications. He is a founding partner of Lost Image Desk, a visual research firm in San Francisco and New York.

He is author and coauthor of numerous books. His most recent book, *American Trademarks, A Compendium*, was published in 2010 by Chronicle Books of San Francisco in July, 2010.

For the past 20 years Eric has taught at the School of Visual Arts in Manhattan.

A two time recipient of the National Endowment for the Arts Design Grant for his independent design history projects, his work has appeared in *Print, Communication Arts, How, Domus, Metropolis, Blueprint, ID Magazine, The New York Art Directors Annual, British Design and Art Direction, The New York Times, Vanity Fair* and *Graphis*.

A native of California Eric studied at the San Francisco Academy of Art and the California College of Arts and Crafts.

Scrabble story

by Marian Bantjes

I have a lot of long-distance friends, but not so many close-to-home, real-life touchable friends.

A few years ago, one of these non-virtual friends—who I will call "Jim"—told me that he had been playing online Scrabble for a couple of months and that he was feeling pretty confident. Confident enough to take me on. I'm not a Scrabble wizard, but I'm pretty good; I'm also known for being deeply competitive and for my emotional outbursts when I lose. I said, "Sure! When do you want to come over?"

He didn't want to come over. He wanted to play online, through Facebook. I was not yet a member of Facebook and at the time I was highly resistant to becoming one. I thought it was preposterous that I should have to join this stupid online community (in which I am now, years later, deeply entrenched) just to play a game over the internet with one of my few local friends! But I *do* actually live on an island, and Jim was across the water, so I agreed. I joined Facebook.

We were on the phone, and he talked me through how to find the game and join it. He said, "Now I'm going to invite you to a game, and because I started the game, I get to go first." We continued to talk on the phone for a few minutes, and he said, "Okay, I've made my first move, and you're really, really going to hate me, because I've used all seven letters."

"WHAT?!?!" I cried in disbelief, and then I opened the game. Sure enough, he had played NIELLOS.

"What the hell is that?"

He said, "It's a kind of black, used in etching ink."

We rung off, as I contemplated my move. I was devastated by this start, and flabbergasted by the word and the speed that it had been put down. Furthermore one of the letters was a blank, and I know how much harder that makes it to find a word, as your mind has to run through that many more possible interpretations with possible letters.

NIELLOS. I looked it up. Technically you can't pluralize it. Etching? What does Jim know about etching? It's so obscure, and he had made the word *while we were talking on the phone*! Who does this?

I continued to play, and he was playing very well, having already mastered the words running down the sides of other words to make multiple miniwords. Increasingly upset, I started to rave about this to my friends. That evening I went to my friend Peter's house for dinner, and upon hearing my outraged rant, he said "Do you think maybe he's using some kind of online helper?"

I was stunned—it had honestly never occurred to me. "An online Scrabble helper? Do you think there is such a thing?" (I am so naïve.) Peter said, "Let's look!" and went to the computer.

First hit, an online scrabble helper wherein you could type in the letters you had (even set up the board as it was beforehand). I put in Jim's letters, randomly, including the blank.

NIELLOS. The highest possible score for those letters, in the exact position Jim had placed it on the board. I looked at Peter. Peter looked at me. I started putting in some of our subsequent moves, and while I was guessing at Jim's letters based on what he had played, the results were remarkably similar.

I was stunned. But I thought, *well, he's a new player, and he's only ever played online, maybe he doesn't know this would be cheating.* I went home, and wrote in my Facebook status line "Marian is suspicious of the way Jim is playing Scrabble."

Two minutes later the phone rang. Jim says, "Whaddaya mean?"

"Well," I said, "You know ... NIELLOS ... you put it down pretty quick. It's pretty obscure. I just think, maybe... maybe you had a little online help with that."

"I'm really insulted you would think that."

"Well ..."

"No, I'm really pissed off. I would never do that!"

"Okay, if you say so—"

"No. I can't believe this, I can't believe you'd accuse me of cheating!"

"Okay! It's fine, if you say you weren't cheating, then you weren't—"

"No, it's not fine—"

"Oh, come on."

"No. I'm really mad; I'm quitting the game."

"Come on. It's fine. If you say you didn't do it, you didn't do it. Keep playing!"

"No. I'm mad."

He hangs up on me. I call him right back, and he doesn't pick up. I call him later, and it goes through to voicemail, where I leave a message, "Jim, I'm sorry. Really, don't be like this. Call me back."

The next day, I log on to Facebook, where I now have two friends: Jim and—wait a minute. Jim has *unfriended* me! The Scrabble game is gone, and I have only one Facebook friend. I email Jim and apologize again, asking him to call me. He never does.

A month goes by, and this has become my story du jour. I tell it to everyone I meet. No one, not even *very good* Scrabble players, have ever heard of NIELLOS. Everyone, *everyone*, thinks he was cheating. I'm still incredulous—not that he may or may not have cheated—but that he would act this way. That he would discontinue our friendship over something so insignificant. I try again to contact him, to no avail.

Two months later I'm telling the story to Jonathan Hoefler at a conference. On the subject of Scrabble, he says, "I'm what I'd call a good living room player."

"That's a great description; it's how I would describe myself," I say. And thus began my online Scrabble–playing with Jonathan. We were perfectly matched and playing was fun, complete with witty reparté and anguished but lighthearted loss on either side. We continue to play word games online to this day. Meanwhile Facebook took over my life.

But Jim, despite a few more attempts on my part to contact him— including one on New Year's Eve—stayed away, long after I stopped telling the Scrabble Story, until about a year after the event. He came to see me, and we failed to see eye to eye over the incident. It took a long time to get back on good footing with each other again, but we did so only with the understanding that we must never speak of Scrabble again.

NIELLOS, my ass.

....

Marian Bantjes lives and works from an island off the west coast of Canada. She has been variously described as a typographer, designer, artist and writer. Her work has been published in books and magazines around the world, and is included in the permanent collection of the Cooper-Hewitt National Design Museum (Smithsonian) in New York. She is a member of Alliance Graphique Internationale (AGI). In 2010, Thames & Hudson published her book *I Wonder*, and in September 2013 they published a giant monograph of her work, titled *Pretty Pictures*.

Not letting go

by Alex Bogusky

When I was in my early twenties, I spent all of my time at the beach windsurfing. The bigger the wind and the waves, the better. Most days, these sort of conditions keep people off the beach.

But on this spring day it was windy and wavy, *and* unusually sunny and warm. Florida is famous for its undertow, a tidal condition where the water being pushed up on shore creates invisible rivers flowing away from shore. Beach goers get swept out, and in their desperation to swim back the way they came, they fight a losing battle against the rip and eventually tire and slip under the water. (Tip: If you're ever caught in a rip, the best plan is to go with it until it pulls you out past the breakers. Then swim parallel to shore and find a better way in.)

The more water that pushes up on the beach (in the form of waves), the stronger the rip. And on this day the rip was bad. The warning flags were up all along the beach, but hey, it was sunny, how bad could it be?

I was sitting in the sand with my wife, looking out at the surf and waiting for the wind to pick back up so I could go windsurfing. Suddenly we heard a shriek from down the beach. A woman was hysterical and pointing at her son sitting in an inner tube that was getting sucked out through the surf. A group of men ran into the water. Some still in jeans and T-shirts. After a few minutes of commotion, they reached the boy and began to pull him in. But one of the men had been caught in a particularly nasty bit of rip and surf. He was swimming hard but making no progress and with each passing wave it seemed like he surfaced more slowly and with his head just barely above water. I pointed him out to my wife and said that I thought the man was drowning. I stood up and told her that I thought I should go

Photo: Chad Poorman

"

We watched as
60 yards away
this man fought
for his life. And I
felt like a coward.

"

out there and try to get him, but she got angry and reminded me how drowning victims often wind up drowning their rescuers. Which I know is true.

We watched as 60 yards away this man fought for his life. And I felt like a coward.

A wave swept over. He came back up. Another wave. And he came up again. A bigger wave crashed down and he came up. But face down. He certainly wouldn't drown me now. I knew the beach and the currents, and I knew if I tried to reach him from here I'd be swept right past him so I ran up the beach 20 yards and jumped in. I put my head down and swam as fast as I knew how. The rip was taking me out quickly and I popped my head up to try to find him. I was in a good spot to reach him. I put my head down again to just swim. The next time I looked up he was right next to me. As I reached out to grab the back of his tank top and pull him to me, his head was down and the current pushed him deeper. You think odd things at times like this, and I thought, "This guy doesn't care at all. He's not going to be any help." Of course, he couldn't help. He was drowned.

As I flipped him over, his eyes were open and lifeless. I wrapped my arms around his chest and found out he was a big dude—200 lbs. to my 165. This was gonna suck. As I swam with my legs I pumped his chest and started talking to him, telling him to hang on and stay with me. The pumping and squeezing of his chest was doing something and foam started to come out of his mouth.

The problem was that the waves he had been in were the same waves we were both in now, and I was swimming for both of us. Pretty soon it dawned on me that I was starting to drown, too. I knew that if I let go of him I could make it back to shore, but I wasn't sure we both could. A big part of me—maybe the rational part—wanted to let go. But it was impossible. Not impossible as in I couldn't live with myself, but actually physically impossible. My arms would not let go. Later I learned that this phenomena is not uncommon. It's why police officers sometimes end up being pulled off of rooftops by jumpers, and why police are told not to grab jumpers. Because if they do, they probably won't be able to let go.

So all that was left to do was to kick. Keep kicking and praying. I believe we all pray at times like this no matter what we believe the rest of our days. Finally, I kicked and hit something solid. Sand. The bottom. I stood up and started to drag him in. Soon the other men who had rescued the boy reached us and took him from me.

....

The woman who was shrieking earlier was letting out sounds I'd never heard before. The drowned man was her husband.

....

On that day, there had been so many close calls that the paramedics had their trucks moving up and down the beach, and they were there as we pulled the man on shore. They began CPR instantly. I was sick, sad and exhausted so I just walked off to find a quiet place to sit. Within minutes the ambulance and the family were shuttled off. My dad read in the paper the next day that the man had survived. Knowing he was alive and that their family was still together was an indescribable feeling.

Years later, when we launched the Truth® campaign I would feel that feeling again a thousand fold knowing that hundreds of thousands of kids would decide not to smoke because of the advertising we made. Who would have thought you could save more people with an ad than by playing lifeguard.

....

Alex Bogusky's career in communications began over twenty years ago when he joined Crispin and Porter Advertising in 1989 as an art director, eventually running the agency a decade later. Under Alex's direction, Crispin Porter + Bogusky grew to more than 1,000 employees with offices in Miami, Boulder, Los Angeles, London and Sweden, and with annual billings over $1 billion. During Alex's leadership, CP+B became the world's most awarded advertising agency. In 2008, he was inducted into the Art Director's Club Hall of Fame. And in 2010, Alex received the rare honor of being named "Creative Director of the Decade" by *Adweek* magazine.

Always drawn towards a cause, Alex created groundbreaking initiatives such as the Truth campaign, which was named the most successful social advertising campaign in U.S. history. He has worked with Vice President Al Gore to debunk the notion of "clean coal" with TV spots directed by the Coen Brothers. And in 2011, Alex conceived and launched 24 hours of Climate Reality, the most highly viewed streaming web program to date.

Having left CP+B in 2010, he and his wife Ana keep busy helping non-profits with their advertising through their consultancy, The FearLess Revolution. They also mentor social entrepreneurs and start-ups through COMMON^CM, a collaborative network for accelerating social ventures under a unified brand.

In 2012, Alex joined partners Dave Schiff, Scott Prindle and John Kieselhorst as a Partner/Creative Advisor for MadeMovement, a new marketing agency dedicated to the resurgence in American manufacturing.

He lives in Boulder, Colorado with his wife Ana and their two teenage children.

Uranus

by Bonnie Siegler

 My design studio was hired to create the animated logo for MTV Productions, which was the brand new filmmaking arm of MTV Networks. This seventeen-second piece would appear before every movie MTV made, starting with their first cinematic endeavor, *Beavis and Butt-Head Do America*.

Essentially it would be their version of MGM's roaring lion or 20th Century Fox's klieg lights.

Before we were hired we had to go through a pitch process. We showed them about eight different storyboards. Most of them revolved around the "moon man," who had become a mascot for MTV since his introduction in the first moments of MTV. These moments featured the iconic footage of Neil Armstrong during the Apollo 11 moon landing. One of my favorites that they didn't choose involved a kind of Capricorn One story, where we pulled back on the famous image of the moon landing to reveal that it was just a set after all. Each of our solutions had a specially chosen name, a title if you will, that was meant to perfectly encapsulate the big idea. They chose the storyboard called "Uranus."

To this day, I'm almost positive they chose the idea simply because of the name. I mean, these were the people who had brought Beavis and Butt-Head to life. Of course they chose Uranus.

So we got the job. And the idea they chose was very much inspired by the moon man's awesome debut. This time around however, as MTV embarked on this journey into filmmaking, we wanted to send the moon man even further into space in search of new frontiers. We painstakingly searched through NASA footage to see if we could use a real moonwalk as the basis for our piece, but nothing offered exactly what we were looking for.

We would have to shoot it. We found a great soundstage with high enough ceilings. We designed the logo, which was to be reflected in the astronaut's helmet. We created sound effects for the heavy breathing of the astronaut. Everything was perfect. The only remaining obstacle was to get a real astronaut suit, but that wouldn't be that hard, right? Maybe NASA could lend us one? Nope. Rent? There goes our whole budget. The Halloween costumes we came across looked too flimsy to help survive a chilly day. In the end, the only solution was to find a prop guy to make one for us.

He did a terrific job and the suit really looked like the real thing, only a hell of a lot lighter. We hired an acrobat who wouldn't mind being suspended for a couple of hours and we were thrilled that the suit and helmet fit him as well as they did. Snug as a bug in a rug. All systems go.

In the back of my mind there was the slightest worry that we had hired a prop guy instead of a costume designer, but I pushed that worry away.

Take one: Our acrobat drifted across the black background and everything looked great. He was mimicking the whole zero gravity thing perfectly. He looked so light, so graceful, so astronaut-y. But then he drifted a little too far, looked a little too weightless. A little too . . . unconscious.

....

His head slowly dropped and it was clear he had just fainted. Here was the catch: The prop guy hadn't built air holes into the suit.

....

The tiniest amount of oxygen snuck in, but clearly not enough. We were lucky because it was such a short shot. We were also lucky because he was alive. We got the acrobat down and took the suit off and gave him some air and water, but we did only get that first take.

So if you happen to see this particular animated logo, look for the ever so subtle head drop as our moon man nears the left side of the screen. And the moral of the story: Always try to use real NASA footage. It's free!

....

Bonnie Siegler is the founder of the New York design studio, Eight and a Half. Her work has been recognized by AIGA, Art Directors Club, Type Directors Club, the Society of Publication Designers, the

Webby Awards and the Broadcast Design Association. Clients include Brooklyn Public Library, HBO, Random House, The Criterion Collection, Nickelodeon and the Frank Lloyd Wright Foundation. Before Eight and a Half, Bonnie co-founded design studio Number 17 (the name makes sense now, doesn't it?) with partner Emily Oberman. While at Number 17, Bonnie also served as creative director of *Newsweek* after overseeing its complete redesign. Before starting her company in 1993, she worked at MTV Networks and, before that, studied graphic design at Carnegie Mellon University.

A night with Elizabeth Taylor

by Stanley Hainsworth

Life is a tangled freeway with many exits and on ramps. You can choose to try some of these exits that may lead to new adventures or you can keep on the more-traveled path.

The many decisions you make along the way in life lead to the interesting people you meet and the various employment opportunities you may have. All of these of eventually create the person you will become.

Previous to my career as a designer, I studied acting and vowed to continue in that profession until I was, if not a star, at least a rousing success. Since I didn't have a relative in the business, when I first moved to Los Angeles I was destined for a job at Hamburger Hamlet on Sunset and Doheny—the entrance to Beverly Hills. The location meant that every celebrity, or future celebrity, frequented this upscale burger joint. I waited on pretty much every musician, actor, producer, director, writer or wannabe of note: from Johnny Carson to Alice Cooper.

A typical evening in my humble waiter life follows. (Okay, it didn't all happen in one night, but it did happen.)

5:40 P.M.: A striking, beautiful lady sits at my station. I see her first from behind but as I turn the corner and look at her face I see it is Elizabeth Taylor. I loved her as America's sweetheart like many of us did. But these were the, um, well-fed years of her career and she did not disappoint. She is by herself as I take the order pad out of my apron. "One order of Hamlet Chicken Wings with two sides of hot rooster sauce and a side of blue cheese dressing," she instructs me. The Hamlet Chicken Wings are a jumbo-sized but elegant platter of wings, enough to satisfy a party of four. I deliver her order and she proceeds to eat with gusto. She very nicely finishes the whole order and leaves a respectable tip. As far as I can tell she refrains from licking her fingers.

7:10 P.M.: A large, imposing man enters as I stand behind the counter. He comes directly to me and says that he wants to place an order to go. "One Ultimate Hot Fudge Cake with three scoops of vanilla and an extra container of hot fudge and whipped cream."

I say, "Sure, I can get that slice for you." He says, "No, the whole cake please."

As I walk into the back serving area to get a cake off the rack one of the other servers come up to me and whispers, "That's Michael Jackson's bodyguard. His car is out front and Michael's inside it." I deliver the whole three-layer cake and a container of ice cream to him and he leaves me a $100 tip with a nice thanks.

8:15 P.M.: Dean Martin comes in for an after-dinner drink. Each time he orders he says with a wink, "Stanley, my fine man, may I please have another drink, but only half a shot?" Each time he orders a half a shot, with the half-shots repeated over and over for two hours. An hour into the half-shots, Peter Lawford enters the restaurant and joins his fellow member of the Rat Pack. They close the place down with a handsome tip.

10:30 P.M.: I watch them walk out and finish my closing activities, count the tips and leave for my car, hoping I correctly interpreted the street parking signs so I don't find another ticket on my windshield. Fifteen feet down the sidewalk I see a couple of feet and the bottom of a leg sticking out of the bushes. I get closer, spread the bushes apart and look down at Peter Lawford—drunk and passed out in the bushes. I call for help and take care of him until he is on his way for the night.

11:30 P.M.: I get in my car and drive down Sunset Strip past the brightly lit billboards, avoiding the crowds coming out of Whiskey A Go Go, to the corner of Horn where I pull into the Tower Records parking lot and enter the store to spend a respectable portion of my tip money on a stack of albums.

Stanley Hainsworth is the founder of Tether, a group of friends who are passionate about one thing: telling stories that matter. Tether was born from the desire to work on brands that share the desire to create passionate, emotional connections with customers. Everything Tether's team of visionaries, strategists, designers and implementers create tethers back to the core of the brands they partner with.

Previous to founding Tether, Stanley was VP global creative of Starbucks where he oversaw all creative aspects of Starbucks—new products, packaging systems, seasonal promotions, brand campaigns, advertising and collateral materials.

Stanley spent twelve years at Nike as a creative director working on everything from product launches to Niketowns to the Olympics. After Nike, he moved to Denmark to join the Lego Company as their global creative director. There he directed a total visual overhaul of the Lego brand from top to bottom, including packaging, the web, retail and brand stores.

Stanley is a national board member of AIGA, a featured speaker on creativity worldwide and the recipient of awards from *ID Magazine, Communication Arts*, The Library of Congress, *Graphis*, Type Directors Club, HOW International, HOW Regional, NW Design Awards, PRINT International, AIGA National, AIGA Regional, Rosie's, POP Times, Communication Arts Illustration, Retail Interiors (Best International Store and Best Retail Theater) and MAPIC (Best Retail Store).

Make time for the little guys

by Aaron Draplin

The year was 1995, and I was a hungry, scrappy designer/illustrator living and snowboarding in Bend, Oregon, drawing as much as possible and sneaking into the local community college to poach computer time.

That February, a group of buddies let me hop in their backseat for a big snowboarding trade show in Las Vegas. The entire snowboarding universe was there: all of the companies we had looked up to over the years.

The trade shows are where ski shops peruse the upcoming season's gear, and place respective orders. The undercurrent is a rowdy migration of wild-eyed snowboarders, partners, hopefuls, hangers-on, and downright scrubs like myself, lurking, shaking hands and seeing all the new gear. In short, you could meet the owners of the companies, as well as their employees, and even eyeball their professional riders. Stickers were free, and I loaded up a big bag. Cool stuff for a twenty-one-year-old rat!

A favorite snowboard company of mine had a big booth, and we knew a couple of the guys working it. They gave us a tour of the gear and introduced us to their coworkers. One of the fellas was their art director, a renowned designer in the snowboard world. I was so excited. I remember trying to tell the guy my name and what I did, and how much I liked his work. And he couldn't care less. He was annoyed. Distracted. He was pretty caught up in everything, and I know how that goes, but I distinctly remember feeling bummed after meeting the guy. Maybe he was busy? Maybe he didn't like my meatball face? Hard to say.

It's fun meeting your heroes, you know? But this time it hurt.

That little moment taught me something very crucial over the next couple of years: If a kid comes up to you, no matter what the deal, you have to respect the courage it took and make a little time for them.

And I'm here to say I've done just that—for years—navigating this lucky predicament I've been in for a little over a decade.

I've been doing speaking gigs for about four years and am proud to say that as these words go to print, I'll have upwards of around ninety completed gigs! Just incredible. So lucky. And at these talks, I meet young designers in droves, and they come up to me totally freaking out, nervous, excited—and *I make time for each and every one of them*. I'm learning how to calm them down, make them comfortable and hear their story. I was that same kid many, many times—and still am, on so many levels.

House Industries let me in their shop in 1997, and frankly, they were busy as hell and didn't have to do it. They made time for me, and that made me that much more of a fan. For life. I got to see that they were hardworking guys, funny as hell and insanely creative. They did that for me. And now, I do the same for kids at my shop.

In closing, a couple summers back, I got an e-mail from that designer I looked up to so much. He had recently stumbled onto my work and wrote to tell me how much he dug what I was up to—and, to tell me, *if I ever had any extra work, to consider him.*

I'd rather give the work to the kid who came up to me in Rapid City, shaking, and told me, "Draplin, I sent out one hundred resumes, and you were the *only* one who wrote back!" Wow. I felt bad for the kid hearing that. When he wrote me, I commented on his impressive work, gave him a couple pointers and offered up a couple leads in Portland. Small talk, you know? He was moved, and in turn, to see how it helped him, it moved me right back. We hugged it out, and I warned him to stay the fuck out of Portland! Ha!

Make time for the little guys. Always.

....

The Draplin Design Co. is located in the mighty Pacific Northwest. Our proud list of services: graphic design, illustration, friendship, clipping pathery, garying, jokes/laughter, campfire strummin', gocco dynamics, road trip navigation, trust, guitar tuning, gen'l conversation, culture critique, color correcting, existential wondering, bounty hunting, heavy lifting, advice, a warm meal, simple ideas, and occasional usage of big words.

Dead man's suit

by John Sabel

My father was a very conservative guy. That is an undeniable fact. He was a true American hero, bigger than life in every way. Eagle Scout, lifeguard, Golden Gloves boxer, World War II B-17 bomber pilot.

He was there for the start of the CIA, and we found out later he was an agent until 1968. He was a tough, hard-boiled guy, big and imposing. He was a cross between Perry Mason and the Great Santini.

I, on the other hand, was in my second year of junior college and wanted to follow my dreams of being an artist. I was young and impressionable, totally insecure. I guess I was to some extent sheltered; we lived in a small beach town. And I was trying to live up to the huge shadow my dad was casting. My dad wanted me to give up on the art thing and get a degree in dentistry like my uncle. Either that or just give up on college altogether (I wasn't that bright) and go into tool and die as a machinist's apprentice. Car painter would have worked for him, too.

My big break came when a neighbor mentioned that he knew the creative director at an ad agency in downtown Los Angeles. They were looking for summer interns to work in the art department, and he would set up a interview if I was interested. Hell yeah!!!!!

Everything was going great until my dad asked the question: "Are you going to get a haircut?"

"No, I like my hair the way it is," and I thought to myself was he out of his mind.

"What are you planning to wear?"

"What I always wear: blue jeans, work shirt, hiking boots." And, again, I thought he was out of his mind.

Truth was, for the first time in my life my dad was showing a real interest in me and my prospect of a real job. This became that great moment of our first father-and-son talk.

"Look, advertising is a business and if you want to get the job, you have to look and act the part." His confidence and conviction convinced me that he knew how the game was played. "Cut your hair and wear a suit."

I didn't own a suit. And all my money at the time was going into art supplies.

My dad didn't offer to pay for the suit. Instead he told me about Al Rosen, a friend of his that was a great dresser and a very successful lawyer in Beverly Hills.

Then he drops the bomb: Al died two weeks before and he was about my size.

Dad offered to call Al's widow if I wanted and ask her what she was going to do with Al's clothes. I wanted to believe this was a good idea;

that this is what people did for their first job interview and that my
dad was steering me in the right direction.

I drove my mom's Toyota Corolla to a nice big Beverly Hills home
and knocked on the door. Al's widow answered, she still had puffy
red eyes from mourning Al. We walked up stairs into a dark master
bedroom and into the huge walk-in closet that Al had. It was lined
with a ton of beautiful suits and shirts. A slight smell of mildew. She
pulled one suit of the rack and handed it to me and said, "This was
Al's favorite suit." It was the one that he would wear to close his cases.
It was his lucky suit. I tried on the jacket and it fit, except that the
shoulders were a little padded. The pants fit, except for a little pooch
that needed some alteration. She said I looked great, that I looked like
I could sell anything to the world.

She asked if I needed a shirt.

"Yes, that would be great." She gave me one with Al's monogram.
It was a French cuff, and she offered me some gold-plated cuff links
with the Scales of Justice. She gave me a big power tie by a famous
Italian designer.

"What size shoe are you?"

"Ten and a half."

That was Al's shoe size. She pulled out a pair of handmade Alliga-
tor shoes. She wished me luck with my new job. I got home and my dad
wanted to help me with my resume. We went up to his home office and
he got behind the IBM Selectric, slipped in a piece of onionskin paper.

"Name?" he said.

"John Sabel." I couldn't believe he had to ask what my name was.

"Address?" "Previous Experience?" "Hobbies, special interests?"

Single, Caucasian and willing to travel. The resume was finished.
He folded it and put it in an envelope.

The interview day arrived.

I borrowed my mom's Toyota Corolla and drove in stop-and-go
traffic down the 110 freeway. It was a hot morning made hotter by the
fact that Al's suit was made out of wool. I was sweating, soaking wet. I
got to the area where the agency was and then I had to find a parking
space a couple blocks away. I grabbed my portfolio and made my way
to the front of the building. I got in the elevator and looked at everyone in the elevator. I looked better than they did. The doors opened

and I walked to the receptionist. My armpits were soaking wet and my head felt like it was going to explode from the heat.

The receptionist told me to have a seat. The creative director was not in yet. I drank some water and waited. He arrived. He was 6 foot 5 inches, wearing black jeans, black cowboy boots, a black shirt. He had a shaved head and had two silver earrings in his ears. He shook my hand and asked if I was the artist/intern? We sat in his office, and he asked if I was comfortable.

"Yes." I was sweating like a pig!

"Did I always wear a suit?"

"No, this is a dead man's suit."

"What?"

"It's a dead man's suit. My father said that advertising is a business and if you want to get the job, you have to dress the part. You have to look like them. This is Al's suit. He died two weeks ago. Al was a very successful lawyer—this was his favorite suit, his closing suit—look, these are French cuffs with his initials. His cufflinks with the scales of Justice. The shoes are handmade!"

The creative director stared blankly.

"Come on. Let's meet the art directors," he said.

"Hey everybody, this is John. He is an artist. John, tell 'em about the suit."

I did and everyone laughed and liked the suit (I think).

We went back to his office. He looked at my portfolio, and I gave him the resume .

I think that the resume freaked him out a little. He said, "Guess what?"

"What?"

"You don't have to wear a suit again." He liked my work. He laughed at the resume and said that nothing mattered except the work in my book, and he didn't care if I knew how to swim or if I liked to play tennis.

That night at the dinner table, my dad asked me how the interview went.

"I got the job!"

"It was the suit," he said.

To this day, I am a little freaked out about suits. I am tempted to check out the secondhand stores every once in a while, but then, you can never tell what the story is with some of the coats. Were they lucky jackets? Or was the guy who owned it eager to unload it on some unknowing sucker? Or are they just the clothes that the family cleaned out after some guy died?

....

John Sabel is the executive vice president of creative print for the Walt Disney Studios. John and his team have created marketing campaigns for some of the industry's biggest blockbusters in Hollywood history. *The Rock*, *Armageddon*, *Pirates of the Caribbean*, *Up*, *Wall-E*, *Alice in Wonderland*, *Tangled*, *Toy Story 3*, *Brave*, *Wreck-it Ralph*, *The Avengers*, *Iron Man 3*, and *Monsters University* are some of the most memorable.

Peter Beard

by Gail Anderson

I am not a seasoned professional when it comes to drinking, and even in the prime of my youth, could barely finish a bottle of Rolling Rock.

I never developed a taste for alcohol, or strangely enough, for coffee—I've never had a cup. I was, and am, way too earnest for my own good. So it's hard to explain how I ended up sprawled out across the floor of the ladies room at *Rolling Stone* magazine, head poised against the cool white porcelain of the toilet bowl, at five in the morning.

The story we were working on had something to do with endangered elephants, its opening spread filled with an African landscape dotted by tiny collaged pachyderms. The piece was excerpted from photographer Peter Beard's journal. Beard was a striking, wind-blown gentleman in perhaps his midfifties at the time. He was the definition

Photo: Darren Cox

of charm. Beard planted himself in the art department of our office at 745 Fifth Avenue—my department—and set to work with photo prints and tweezers, as he pieced together his complex masterpiece. I could barely get myself to meet his eye as he worked, afraid that I'd break his concentration or just be a pain in the ass staring at a celebrity photographer. In the moment, he might as well have been Hemingway. He was ruggedly cool.

We liked to work late at *Rolling Stone*, as much as we groused about it. Saying that you'd put in a long night was sort of a badge of honor at the magazine, where we cared deeply about every word and every piece of design on the page. It was another long Friday evening in the making. Peter Beard was still in the office, now on deadline so we could close his African elephant journal on Saturday morning when the design, production and copy departments would return to work. We were hungry, and Beard suggested we order Japanese food. And sake.

During my early tenure at *Rolling Stone*, I'd become acquainted with sake bombs, a concoction that involved mixing sake and Sapporo by dropping a small cup of sake into a tall glass of beer. As I said, I wasn't much of a drinker when I started at the magazine, but I enjoyed the mix of the two flavors and the warm buzz that followed. There were three of us working late with Beard that night; Geraldine, a budding designer and assistant to Fred Woodward, our illustrious art director, and Lee, a studious, clever designer from California. I was with two of my favorite people and in the company of a fancy photographer who had once been married to supermodel Cheryl Tiegs (I learned this from a television commercial).

These were heady days in magazine publishing, filled with large budgets, fully catered dinners and little amenities such as personalized notepads.

....

Sushi was expensed in plentiful quantities that evening, and the makings of a modest number of sake bombs arrived in tow.

....

Our guest soon became our host, and Beard suggested we call in a few more plastic containers of sake to last through the work night.

Several deliveries later, and after the consumption of many sake bombs, Beard appeared to be less interested in the sake-bombing process than he was in the straight sake drinking process. We obliged. The plastic take-out container tops became excellent makeshift Frisbees, and the containers themselves, building blocks and targets. The warm sake started to taste pretty darned good without the beer, and several more orders followed. We listened to music, and as the night progressed, decided it would be even more fun to sing along. We created new games to play with the empty sake containers. The view from the 23rd floor of our Fifth Avenue office was spectacular, and we were mesmerized by our new drinking buddy, Peter Beard. Oh wait, where was he? Beard was gone by midnight, leaving us completely inebriated.

Well, who needed him anyway? The cleaning ladies were gone, and we had an entire empty office to play in. The hallways were long, so it seemed like a good idea to create a bowling alley and knock down a few more sake containers. Paper planes were flown across Central Park— our office windows actually opened even though we were pretty high up. We were young, drunk and hanging out our 23rd floor windows while we sang into the night sky. Luckily, none of us thought we could fly.

My cohorts and I made our way down the office hall using container tops as paving stones. Pictures appeared to be crooked on walls, but we had no idea how they got that way. Papers flew from desktops. It was late, and Geraldine and I knew we'd be losing Lee to his girlfriend soon. We were hot and tired, and needed to cool down a bit before sending him home. The ladies room seemed like a good place to rest, since there was a small leather couch by the mirror. Lee had never visited our respite before and was taken aback by its superiority to its masculine counterpart. The black-and-white tile floor was freshly washed and cool to the touch—we'd been reduced to hands and knees by this point. One of my last memories was of one of us purring, "This tile feels good," as we lay across the floor, and a chant of, "Oh, toilet bowl."

When Geraldine and I woke up, Lee was gone. It was down to just us die-hard girls. I could barely open my eyes as I made my way back around the hall towards my office, picking up strewn papers and sake containers, and straightening pictures on walls. It was almost morning, and we needed to sleep just a bit more before our coworkers began to arrive for the Saturday magazine closing. When I awoke again, I was on the couch in my office, and Geraldine was stretched out across my floor, looking no worse for the wear.

It was now about 8:30 A.M., and we had to be ready to work by 10. I needed to go home to take a shower before starting the day. Geraldine flipped her hair back, put on her Ray Bans, and smiled. "That was fun," she said. "I'll see you later." She darted off to the subway, seemingly fresh as a daisy, and I slowly made my way across town, back to my apartment on 65th Street.

Fred was among the first to arrive when I returned to the office at 10, bleary-eyed, but freshly washed. "Why are there paper planes in my office?" he asked. Busted!

Gail Anderson is a designer, writer, and educator. From 2002 through 2010, Anderson served as creative director of design at SpotCo, creating artwork for Broadway and institutional theater. From 1987 to early 2002, she worked at *Rolling Stone*, as designer, deputy art director, and finally, as the magazine's senior art director. She is coauthor, with Steven Heller, of *New Modernist Type*, as well as *New Ornamental Type* and *New Vintage Type*. Anderson is a contributor to Imprint, *Print* magazine's design blog, and she has taught at the School of Visual Arts for over 20 years. She is the recipient of the 2008 Lifetime Achievement Medal from the AIGA, and the 2009 Richard Gangel Award from the Society of Illustrators.

The occupant

by Vanessa Eckstein

Once, when we were moving from New York to Los Angeles and making the journey by car, my husband and I found ourselves running out of gas late at night on the back roads of New Mexico.

It was on this road of abandoned towns where missionaries had set up and then left hundreds of years ago that we found ourselves with no options other than to stay at the only "OTL" we could find and solve the gas situation in the morning.

I say "OTL" and not "MOTEL" because the "M" and the "E" on the establishment's sign were nowhere to be found. It was a place so clichéd and generic that I do not even remember if it had a name.

A long row of rooms without a single car parked in front of them was not a convincing image of superior quality and service, but we did not have a choice and simply parked our overstuffed, khaki-colored Jeep Wrangler at the side of the small house that functioned as reception.

We entered a room of scruffy furniture and dirty carpets. No one was there. A cigarette burned in a heavily used ashtray, creating an eerie haze of smoke, while an ancient black and white TV hummed its news in the corner. A black cat slunk around the corner, gave us a desultory glance, and continued on its way.

After many, many minutes, an extremely old woman shuffled into the office. Without speaking, she handed us a sheet of dusty paper to register for our room. We filled in the required details and the woman handed over the motel key. But as we turned to leave, she shouted, "Your description of the car and driver's license."

Surprised, we asked why she needed this information. "In case you are murdered or go missing the next day," she answered.

To say that we found her comment odd was an understatement. It was downright freaky. But we had been driving for six days and all seems a little off when you are tired. However, we did our best to ignore our feelings and headed towards our car.

Just then, a black Crown Victoria glided into the space beside the Jeep. It stopped, and a man emerged from the driver's side. He was dressed head to toe in black, and carried a silver metal briefcase. He stood, silently, looking at us from behind dark sunglasses.

Alarmed, we drove to our room. Opening the door, we were greeted by the two missing letters of OTL, the "M" and the "E", lying haphazardly on our bed. Had I had more vision, I would have simply kept these beautiful typographical relics and included them in the collection of old letters I now own. But I was young and very honest then, so we took them back to the old woman at reception. How very strange it was to find the man in black, still clutching his metal brief-case, talking to the old woman about us. We said nothing, and handed over the letters. As we turned to go back to our room he spoke. "So you are in transition?" he asked.

"

Surprised, we asked why she needed this information. 'In case you are murdered or go missing the next day,' she answered.

"

By now we were completely unnerved. We muttered a few incoherent words, and quickly left. As we unlocked our room, the black Crown Victoria drove up and parked right next to our Jeep. The man in black got out carrying the silver briefcase.

This was pre-cell, pre-laptop, pre-GPS, pre-everything that would connect us with the rest of the world. No one knew where we were. We looked at each other, retreated into our room, locked it, then took all of our bags and piled them against the door. As if this would have stopped anyone from breaking the huge glass window that looked out into the parking lot and was so typical of these motels.

We spent the night visualizing every possible death scenario, my mother's reaction, the old lady's testimony, the newspaper headlines and the photographs of our bodies splayed across the front page.

We never asked ourselves why the man in black would do it, what his motive would be. In that moment, in that mindset, it had for us all the disturbing traits of a Hitchcock plot and truly felt inevitable.

Naturally, morning and dawn brought our irrational fantasies to a sensible halt. Of course nothing happened. Of course we were perfectly fine—rattled and exhausted from lack of sleep, but in one piece. We left at first light and never looked back. It was a poetic reminder of a simple rule: never let fear get the best of you, either in life or work. You'll have far fewer sleepless nights!

Vanessa Eckstein is founder and principal of Blok Design, a graphic design firm she launched in 1998. Having lived and worked in Buenos Aires, LA, New York, Mexico City and Toronto, she brings a unique international perspective and insight to each project, whether that's developing brand identities and experiences or designing and publishing books. She has collaborated with highly talented thinkers from around the world, from architects to contemporary artists to writers, taking on initiatives that blend cultural awareness, a love of art, and humanity to advance society and business alike.

In 2008, she founded a publishing company, collaborating with some of the leading contemporary artists of our time to create children's books designed to foster a life-long relationship with contemporary art, as well as publishing books designed to be a catalyst for positive social change.

Vanessa is a frequent speaker at design symposiums from Latin America to the US and Canada, and has served as judge on numerous international awards shows. She was vice-president of the Association of Registered Graphic Designers in Canada and has taught at the Ontario College of Art and Design in Toronto. She currently sits on the board of the Art Directors Club of Canada.

Vanessa's work has received accolades and awards from around the world. She has been published in *Masters of Design*, Gestalten's "Echoes of the Future", *One by One*, and *Source Book of Contemporary Graphic Design*, and has been written up in *Dwell Magazine*, *Wallpaper* and *Azure* among others. Her work has been exhibited in museums from Japan to Toronto and is part of the permanent collection of the Royal Ontario Museum.

Vanessa holds an MFA from the Art Centre of Pasadena.

How I learned to fear ducks

by Christian Helms

I'd only been in Texas a few months when I found myself in the backseat of an unfamiliar speeding vehicle, soaked and reeking of booze while a screaming man waved a pistol from the truck's open front window.

After growing up in a small mill town in North Carolina, I had spent the past year having my young spirit crushed by New York. In desperation I'd decided to move to a town that I knew I'd love to live in—job or no job. That town was Austin, Texas. Everyone had told me that by leaving the city I was throwing away my career, so I thought I could at least enjoy some queso and cheap beer while I figured out my next life's work in retail sales, llama farming or the Texas Senate.

I was lucky to land an entry-level design gig at a great growing ad firm in town. I was green. I was young-ish. I was eager to prove my worth and to *experience* Texas. So when one of the principals asked who might be up for a pet project, I jumped at the chance. To be clear, I had absolutely no idea what I was volunteering for. I might have been slightly hungover. But I was showing enthusiasm, and that was important.

The project was to build the brand identity and sales materials for a hunting resort on the Texas coast. The owner, Bob Brass, was a wealthy good ol' boy who was a friend of my boss. He was exactly what you'd imagine a ninth-generation Texan named Bob Brass would be. Not a subtle guy.

The resort worked like this: Pay for a weekend at the ranch, and hunt as much as you like. But you pay for what you shoot, and prices vary. So you can "jam econo" and shoot a ton of boar for bargain basement prices, or you can scale up the value ladder and bag a blackbuck antelope, zebra or wildebeest. It's your world to kill as you can afford.

I drove three hours to the coast with Molly, a new account services team member who must've volunteered as well. Our conversation revolved around figuring out where we were and the nagging suspicion that this was an elaborate initiation prank. We were to meet a photographer in the morning to shoot the ranch.

We arrived and Bob Brass immediately greeted us. Powerful handshake. Slap on the back. Boisterous laugh that made you feel like family. That was for Molly. Then he looked at me. I can only describe his expression as if I'd shorted him fries at the drive-through. I was unsure and slightly anxious, and Bob could smell it. He instructed us to leave our bags in the car and immediately loaded us into a fan boat— or "swamp sled" as he called it. Although nervous, I was determined be full of enthusiasm. "Let's do this!" I said.

Bob announced with a commanding yawp that he was showing us around the coastal portions of the property as the sunset and that he'd be piloting the boat. Upon hearing that, the crew immediately exited the vehicle. "Hold onto your hats, ladies!" he screamed over the roar of the fan, as my favorite baseball cap disappeared into the distance.

I learned a few things about fan boats in the forty-five minutes that followed. My first opportunity for education was when Bob jumped a berm of land in an attempt to go airborne and sunk the fan portion of the boat deep into the marsh. As Bob restarted the engines and throttled them at full power to right the boat, I watched the crew cheer with great spirit from the docks. *Give it hell, Bob!* I thought.

I later learned that they were not cheering but panicking. Bob's maneuver was a pretty big no-no in swamp-sled piloting circles—because it often results in violently flipping the boat and breaking the necks of everyone onboard. Lucky for me, I had no idea. Onward!

Bob Brass didn't waste time once we were back in action, and he took to powering around corner blinds of marshy reeds to surprise native wildlife. The diversity of animals he terrorized was impressive. We startled pelicans, whooping cranes, geese and a host of ducks. I was not aware a heron's eyes could grow so large so quickly or that their faces could convey such a range of emotion.

The boat was fast. Plenty fast enough to keep pace with whatever frightened flock of waterfowl Bob set his sights on traumatizing. It's odd how repetition can breed familiarity, and I quickly got used to watching ten to twenty birds flying together around the boat at their top speed. They moved together in a seamlessly choreographed formation and the boat followed. Fowl and watercraft banked and sliced across the coastline in tandem—them through the air and us through the water. It was actually beautiful, I thought, even though the ducks were constantly looking over their shoulders in frenzied alarm. But still, it was almost mesmerizing. My posture relaxed. I exhaled. I leaned back and raised my eyes to take in the sunset.

It was at that moment that a duck shit directly into my mouth.

So there's a lot you think about when a duck shits in your mouth at sixty miles per hour. Your first thought is, as I experienced it, *Did I just get punched in the face? Hard?* And then, *By shit?* The answer across the board was a resounding yes. Yes, I did.

Fun fact: At that speed, when feces hits your face, it doesn't really matter if your mouth is closed. The sheer velocity of the projectile poop forces it through your pursed lips and across your teeth, leaving a brackish, silty coating all the way past your molars and into the back of your throat. And it happens quickly. Still, I thought, maybe no one saw it and if I maintained my enthusiasm, I could avoid a scene.

I might have thrown up in the boat.

The sun set and we retired to our rooms—Molly with her notes for the following day, and me with four bottles of water and a toothbrush. We had a 4 A.M. call for a sunrise photo shoot of coastal sportsmanship.

The following day was brutal. In the freezing water by 5 A.M. to set up shots and catch the good light at sunrise, then inside for interior shots until 7 P.M. and then back outside to shoot a festive sportsman BBQ at sunset. By 9 P.M., the photographer, Molly and I were exhausted.

But our trip was nowhere near done. The work was through, and now Bob Brass wanted to make us his famous margaritas and show us the ranch land. "I'm psyched. Let's do this," I said, with less enthusiasm than the prior day. We each downed a sixteen-ounce cocktail that was, by far, mostly liquor, and climbed into a Chevy Suburban with spotlights mounted to the top— or as Bob called it, Ranch-Hawg. Bob was going to ~~traumatize~~ show us some wildlife.

The ranch trails were bumpy and it was nighttime, so we saw no axis deer and we managed to slosh and spill our Brass-a-Ritas all across the interior of Bob's Suburban. In an attempt to spare the upholstery, I threw most of mine onto my neck. There were too few animals to terrorize, and Bob was getting progressively more frustrated, and also more drunk. He piloted us back to the resort for a refill and exited the vehicle while still in motion as he slammed on the parking break. We screeched to a halt. Half out of the vehicle and at a near split, Bob announced that Molly would drive from there on out.

The rest of the evening is still a bit of a blur, but there are a few things I remember. I recall Bob instructing Molly to hold his drink with her knees while driving at top speed. I remember him leaning across her from the passenger side seat with surprising agility, firing his pistol out of the driver's side window at teams of wild boar who were clearly questioning their choices in life. I remember Molly ducking the hot casings as she steered, eyes as big as pie plates. And I recall looking across the bench seat in the back of the suburban at our photographer, who was mouthing the phrase "fucking uncool" over and over again. Determined to keep it together, I beamed back at the photographer with what I had hoped looked like boundless enthusiasm.

I might have thrown up in Ranch-Hawg.

The following morning we loaded up early, awkwardly and likely still drunk. I'm pretty sure that any sign of enthusiasm had fully waned by this point, but I had *experienced* Texas. And people, let me say this: compared to Texas, New York is a pussy.

....

Christian Helms is the founder of Helms Workshop, a strategic design and brand development studio. He's also the co-owner of Frank restaurant, a mecca for beer guzzlers and encased-meat. His clients range from national brands Pabst Brewing, Hasbro and Jack Daniel's, to Texas standouts Alamo Drafthouse Cinema and Austin Beerworks, as well as a host of bands including Spoon, Modest Mouse, The Hold Steady and Wilco.

Christian's work has received international recognition, publication and awards, and he lectures across the country. He's even been awarded a gold record from the Recording Industry Association of America, despite being unable to carry a tune. He lives in South Austin with his wife Jenn, son Hatley, and Boston-Pug mutt ScatterBug.

They made me a criminal

by Jeffrey Zeldman

The jail door slammed, and I was left in a women's holding cell with seven teenage girls. There were no benches so we sat on the floor. I was fifteen but looked twelve.

With long hair on my head and not a whisker to my chin, I resembled a homely girl, although the plainclothes officer who frisked me could have verified otherwise.

They'd picked us up in Point State Park after observing us pass a joint. They'd intended to bust a big dealer named Lonnie—a white guy with long red hair. Fortunately for Lonnie but unfortunately for us, a white guy named John also had long red hair, also happened to be in the park and also happened to possess and publicly share a joint.

I was there after trying to find a summer job selling hotdogs at Three Rivers Stadium. Ten thousand other boys my age had had the same idea that day. Possibly a dozen of them landed a job. My friend Mike and I did not. It was a hot day, and after waiting in line for three hours to fill out a job application, we were ready to go home. But first we had to pick up Mike's friend Donny, who was tripping in Point State Park.

Donny was our age but looked eighteen. His dad was in the Mob. There were guns in his house. Mike looked up to him the way I looked up to Mike.

Mike and I found Donny sitting in a circle with a bunch of teenage girls and a red-haired guy resembling Ian Anderson of Jethro Tull. We were tired, and they were girls so we sat with them. Someone passed a joint and I pretended to smoke it so nobody would know how uncool I was. Moments later a half-dozen men in suits and dark sunglasses burst from the bushes like clowns from tiny cars and began frisking and collaring us. Nobody tried to run away. It took a while to realize these guys were cops. A man in a hat made me stand up, then felt my balls. I asked if he was gay and he hit me in the face. After that, I didn't say anything.

We rode downtown in the back of a genuine paddy wagon. It must have been more fun, or scarier, for the kids who were actually high.

The officer who separated us by sex put me in the women's cell, which was good with me. We were the cell's only occupants; the girls and I hung out playing with matches, learning each other's names and wondering what our parents would do to us if we ever saw them again.

A few months before this, I'd been picked up for shoplifting. I hadn't actually done the shoplifting—my friend Paul had. I didn't even know he'd taken anything. But the salesgirls at J.C. Murphy's hated Paul and me, and the cops believed their story, so I now had a juvenile record in my parents' suburb and was about to get one in Pittsburgh for drug use.

I'd spent the previous year getting beaten up for moving to Pittsburgh from somewhere else, and for being Jewish, and for being small, and for having no facial hair, and for not knowing how to fight, and for not swearing, and for not stealing, and for not smoking, and for sucking at gym, and for raising my hand in class, and for knowing the answers to the teacher's questions. Now I was a delinquent and almost nobody picked on me. Maybe there was an alternate path out of being the class punching bag, but, if so, nobody had clued me in.

There was a little window in the jail door, just like the ones you see on television. After a few hours a lady cop appeared in it and began taking everyone's information. I was the last one to go to the window. The lady cop asked my religion and I said none. She didn't like that, although it probably explained things in her mind. She shut the jail door window when she left.

Two minutes later she was back with a male cop—a huge black guy named Tiny, who made me leave the cell and follow him. During the jail door window interview, I'd given my name. I guess somebody had looked twice at it and realized I was a guy. Tiny escorted me to the cell where they were holding John, Mike and Donnie. I joined them and the door closed. We all watched Donnie come down from his acid trip. It didn't look like fun.

My father cut my hair short and grounded me for two months. He cut it himself with a hair cutting kit he'd bought at the drugstore in the town we'd lived in before Pittsburgh. The box the kit came in said "Cut Hair At Home and Save!"

We were tried as a group in juvenile court. My parents and Mike's parents attended. Donny's dad did not. Before the trial, my lawyer instructed me not to deny I'd smoked pot because nobody would believe me. I was to plead emotional instability and request probation on the grounds of being from the suburbs. Right before our trial began, they sentenced a fourteen-year-old black kid to six months in a juvenile detention center for stealing chewing gum.

....

I stood up. I don't know what I intended to do. Yell at the judge for being racist, I think.

....

My dad grabbed my hand and pulled me back to my seat. I could see in his eyes that he was afraid for me. That made it real.

Happy ending for the white kid from the suburbs: As part of a plea bargain, my parents agreed to send me to a psychiatrist. I was given a year's detention and forbidden to enter Point State Park.

I started using drugs the next day. If I had a record, I was going to live up to it.

....

Dubbed "King of Web Standards" by *Business Week*, Jeffrey Zeldman founded and is chairman of Happy Cog™, a high-end design studio with offices in Philadelphia, Austin, and New York, and has published A List Apart Magazine "for people who make websites" since 1998. He has written two books, notably the foundational text, *Designing With Web Standards*, currently in a 3rd Edition coauthored with Ethan Marcotte. It has been translated into 15 languages and is credited with converting the web design industry from tag soup and Flash to semantics and accessibility.

Jeffrey cofounded the multicity web design conference An Event Apart with Eric Meyer; with Mandy Brown and Jason Santa Maria he cofounded the publishing house A Book Apart, responsible for such groundbreaking titles as *Responsive Web Design* (Ethan Marcotte), *Design Is A Job* (Mike Monteiro), *Mobile First* (Luke Wroblewski), and *Content Strategy For Mobile* (Karen McGrane).

He hosts weekly design podcast *The Big Web Show* (twice winner of *.net Magazine* Podcast of the Year), and is a faculty member on the MFA, Interaction Design program at School of Visual Arts. In 2012, Jeffrey Zeldman was the first human inducted into the SXSW Interactive Hall of Fame.

With Warhol

by Jennifer Morla

As art director for Levi Strauss & Co. in 1983, I was responsible for creating all nonadvertising print materials: mainly catalogs, labeling, posters and the occasional environmental installation.

It was the last days of the disco era, with past Levi's customers opting for Calvin's. I proposed creating a poster and advertising series of famous artists to appeal to our more mature Levi's customer. This did not go over so well with Levi's advertising agency, which trashed the idea (perhaps because it wasn't theirs). This was a couple years before Absolut Vodka launched their famous artist series campaign, an enormous success because they understood the appeal of art—and artists—to their audience.

My list of artists to contact was brief: Andy Warhol, Robert Rauschenberg and David Hockney, with the request for them to interpret the iconic Levi's Jean. With Bob Haas's blessing (president of LS&Co. at the time), I premiered the series with Warhol. Starting with Warhol was a no-brainer: Not only did most everyone know him, he was easy to get a hold of directly. His number was listed in the Manhattan phone book.

I called, Fred Hughes answered and the commission for the silkscreened canvas was set. Soon after, I got a call from Andy himself, saying that he would be sending some Polaroids of his ideas. The photos arrived, and, with excitement, I opened the envelope and saw nine images with Levi's famous button fly unbuttoned with varying degrees of, well, exposure.

The tenth Polaroid was the tamest, with the button fly buttoned. Suffice to say, the marketing execs went for the buttoned-up version.

When I informed Andy that we needed to use the tamest image, he not only understood but invited me to The Factory the following

Photo: Jock McDonald

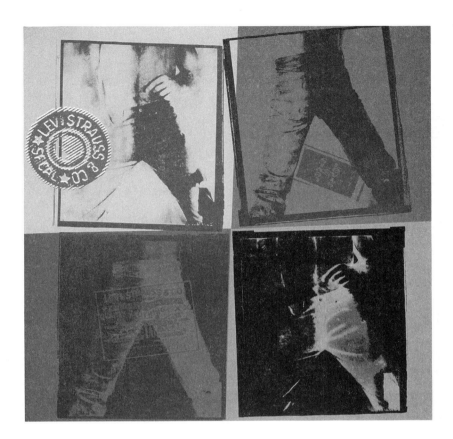

week to see the silk-screening in progress. Very thrilling, especially since I had followed his work and his creative, messed-up coterie of characters since the late 1960s.

Brigid Berlin greeted me upon arrival, and I was asked to join Andy for lunch. International art dealers, various society women, Warhol (and his wild wig) were seated at a large table in a coffered-ceiling dining room with animal trophies hanging on the wood paneled walls. There were perhaps eight of us, and I, being twenty-seven, was by far the youngest one there.

After lunch, with the other guests departed, Warhol asked if I would like to help him chose the ink colors for the canvas. We spent a couple of hours together as his assistant screened the image.

I was invited back the following day to see the finished pieces, which were drying next to the recently screened image of Michael Jackson (as I recall, *Thriller* was the album of the moment, although no favorite of mine). I thanked him for his beautiful work and for inviting me to be a part of the experience. He smiled, went to a desk, took out a copy of his book, *The Philosophy of Andy Warhol*, signed it and gave it to me.

I left Levi's later that year to open Morla Design. As for the risqué Polaroids: I was told by a Levi's marketing director that they were mistakenly tossed a few months later in a department move.

Jennifer Morla is president and creative director of Morla Design, San Francisco, a multidisciplinary firm established in 1984. With over 300 awards of excellence, Morla Design's work has been recognized by virtually every organization in the field of visual communication. She has created major branding programs for companies and non-profits such as Levi Strauss, Wells Fargo Bank, Herman Miller, Capp Street Project, and the Mexican Museum.

Jennifer's work is part of the permanent collections of MoMA, SFMoMA, and the Smithsonian Museum. She has been honored with solo design exhibitions at SFMoMA and the DDD Gallery in Japan. She lectures internationally, teaches at California College of the Arts, and is the recipient of graphic design's most honored award, the AIGA Medal. She is currently an invited artist at The Workshop Residence.

Pignewt

by Charles S. Anderson

I grew up in Boone, a small, remote farm town near the center of Iowa. When I was seven years old, my dad brought home a small dog.

She was a strange-looking creature and seemed completely oblivious to how homely she was. My mom used to say, "She's so ugly, she's cute!" Dad told us she was a Boston terrier.

We named her Frisky, but her nickname was Pignewt. She had a flat face. Half of it was white and half was black, topped off by two pointy ears that stood perpetually at attention. The only relief on her perfectly flat face was a pair of bugged-out eyes. She resembled the giant African vampire bats we looked up in our *Encyclopaedia Britannica* set.

Pignewt didn't realize she was a dog, but rather she considered herself the fourth Anderson sibling. She had free reign over the town of Boone and roamed wherever she pleased. She was an affable pup and nearly everyone in town knew her by name. She spent most of her time with me and my brothers, as we explored the cemetery across the street from our house and the woods beyond.

One blistering day in July, when I was nine years old, I took a shortcut through the woods on my way home from the Dairy Queen. I could see our house just beyond the wall of hedges that marked the cemetery's border. As I stepped into the shadow of a towering 100-foot oak tree, I heard a chattering sound coming from the branches far above. My eyes, adjusting to the shadow, made out the shape of a large gray squirrel. He was extremely agitated and was squealing and chattering with erratic, convulsing movements. I yelled back, "Shut up, you crazy squirrel."

He let out a sick squeal and leaped kamikaze style out of the tree, directly at me. Unfortunately (for him), he wasn't a flying squirrel. He ended his ten-story leap with a disturbing splat on the hot asphalt road about twenty feet short of me. I thought for sure the flattened varmint was done for. Picking up a broken tree branch, I walked forward to inspect the rodent's lifeless carcass. I poked it with the stick—not even a twitch. I bent closer and poked it again. With a shrill, deafening squeal, the squirrel sprang to life, its yellow rat-like teeth gnashing at the air as it lunged for my face. In that split-second glimpse, I saw its blood-red eyes filled with an insatiable evil bred of pure insanity. White foam sprayed out of its mouth like a can of Reddi-wip with a broken nozzle.

I realized this was no ordinary squirrel but a deadly, venomous, rabid squirrel! I blocked the creature's leap with the branch, and in the same gesture spun around and ran for the wall of hedges. Glancing back, I saw that the squirrel was after me ... and gaining! Panicked fear gripped me as I sprinted for the hedge. With a surge of strength fueled by a flood of terror-induced adrenaline, I hurdled the green leafy wall. At that instant the rabid squirrel also sprang, flying through the air, and landed on my shoulder.

"

At that moment
I knew I would die,
and not a good or
heroic death, but
a horribly painful
and embarrassing
death by squirrel.

"

Time shifted into slow motion. I could smell the squirrel's putrid hot breath on my neck and feel the spray of foam and blood from his wretched diseased mouth. I knew those infectious gnawing yellow fangs were just inches from my pounding jugular vein.

At that moment I knew I would die, and not a good or heroic death, but a horribly painful and embarrassing death by squirrel. Just then my peripheral vision detected a blaze of black and white flying through the green hedge. It was Pignewt! She ripped the squirrel off my neck in midair and landed hard on the ground. Suddenly the squirrel was on top of her with a ferocity spawned by disease. The rabid vermin bit a bloody chunk out of Pignewt's neck.

This action triggered thousands of years of repressed bulldog killer instinct. Pignewt surged forward, jaws chomping down with an audible crunch and locking on the squirrel's puny neck. A dozen violent shakes of the dog's massive bulldog neck ensured the multiple snapping of the squirrel's scrawny spine. Not content to simply kill the filthy, bushy-tailed rat, Pignewt began to chow down on the squirrel guts, pulling out its stringy innards and eating them. "Yes!" I yelled. "Good dog! Eat that sick rodent. Rip his guts out!"

Minutes later my mom was rushing me, Pignewt, and the dead squirrel (in a zip lock bag) to the veterinarian. The fact that Pignewt was bleeding profusely did not dampen the dog's buoyant spirits. After all, she had just fulfilled her destiny by not only protecting me but also tearing apart the nasty little beast foolish enough to think he could take a bite out of her and live to tell the tale. Dr. Sandberg was a distinguished, silver-haired, serious-minded veterinarian. He gave Pignewt twelve stitches and then examined the dead squirrel. "Yes," he said, "that confirms it. In my forty-three years of practice, I have never witnessed a squirrel quite this rabid." Then he turned to me, placed his hand on my shoulder, and said, "Son, this dog may very well have saved your life!" I could hear trumpets blowing and angels singing as the clouds of squirrel heaven parted, forming a backdrop for a victorious Pignewt sitting on a golden throne made of dried rabid squirrel carcasses.

Because Pignewt had already been vaccinated for rabies, she suffered no ill effects. She wore her neck bandage proudly, and her heroic status grew daily as the rabid squirrel story spread like a grass fire throughout the small town. According to my friends, she had achieved a place of fame and stature shared only by the likes of Lassie, Rin Tin Tin and Benji.

....

Established in 1989, Charles S. Anderson Design specializes in identity development, packaging, and product design, and is among the world's most influential design firms. Unlike other design firms, however, in addition to their highly-recognized client work, CSA Design is unique in creating what has become one of the most extensive and well-respected archives of licensable artwork in existence. Painstakingly created over many decades, the CSA Images collection is a digital museum of art for commerce, a vast and ever-expanding resource of illustration inspired by the entire visual history of art, design, and typography.

Charles S. Anderson Design Company's work has been exhibited in museums worldwide including The Permanent Collection of The Museum of Modern Art, New York; The Nouveau Salon des Cent–Centre Pompidou, Paris; The Smithsonian Institution's Cooper-Hewitt National Design Museum, New York; The Institute of Contemporary Arts, London; The Library of Congress Permanent Collection, Washington D.C.; The Museum Für Gestaltung, Zürich; The Museum Für Kunst und Gewerbe, Hamburg; The Bibliothèque nationale de France, Paris; The Museum of Modern Art, Hiroshima; and The Museum of Contemporary Art, Shanghai.

The firm's work has also been featured in numerous prominent publications including *The New York Times, In Style, Dwell, Fortune, Rolling Stone, Esquire, Time, Forbes, Entertainment Weekly, Newsweek, Vanity Fair, GQ, The LA Times,* and *ReadyMade.*

CSA Design has been awarded top honors in every major design competition, including multiple gold pencils from The One Show and multiple gold and silver awards from the New York Art Directors Club.

Found in translation

by Debbie Millman

Several years ago I spent a week in Tokyo observing Japanese consumers articulate their feelings about mouthwash and a potential new package design.

It seems absurd, really, to describe my role in this qualitative market research as an observer; it is much more precise to say that I was a listener. I stood rapt with attention as a young woman translated into English what these unusually loyal mouthwash users were saying in Japanese.

Her interpretations were remarkably creative, comprising such statements as "the packaging looks lonely" and "the design is like a

fluffy painting." I couldn't help but wonder if her surprising pro-
nouncements were the verbatim decoding of what was being said or
the result of an imaginative reconstruction.

I'll never know. Being in a country where the language and the
alphabet were both foreign and unreadable reminded me forcefully
of my reliance on language and reading to communicate and relate.
The experience underscored how dependent I am on the ability to
decipher signs in order to distinguish whether my destination is
joyfully welcoming or dreadfully dangerous, and to reassure me
that I know where I am going. While in Tokyo, I was humbled by my
utter disconnection from all such guideposts.

I have been thinking about the inadequacy of language and
interpretation. What is language, really? Why is it that sounds
have come to embody meaning? How accurate are those meanings?
These are basic questions of the philosophy of language. And language, like design, is a system of signs used to communicate. The
act of communicating is a matter of letting other people know what
we think or, in many cases, what to think. The signs that make up
language get their meaning from the ideas we associate with them
and our collective agreement about these associations.

John Locke, the great British philosopher, believed that thought
originates in experience—not in language. Ideas develop as the product of experience, and through this *power of association*, ideas are
transformed into complex mental constructs like language.

But language is a highly arbitrary and highly interpretive
medium. Back when I was about ten or eleven years old, I went
through a particularly difficult phase in my life, when my behavior,
in reflecting on it now, could be best described as characterized by
post-traumatic stress disorder. As a result of the disruption of my
outer world, my inner world began to crumble and I developed a
bizarre speech dysfunction. Whenever anyone asked me how I was
doing, or what the weather was like, or any other innocuous question, I froze. I couldn't answer.

Inasmuch as I thought I knew how I was doing or what the
weather was like, I felt that I couldn't be absolutely sure. What if my
idea about how I was doing wasn't real? What if the weather was different somewhere else? As I tried to answer these benign questions,
I found that all I could muster were responses such as, "Well, maybe

I am feeling well, but maybe I am not," or, "Maybe it is raining, but maybe it is not." "Maybe or maybe not" became my standard reply to any question.

My mother and stepfather were horrified and angry at my inability to articulate an answer to the simplest of questions, and I was punished for my lack of conviction and clarity. But for the life of me I couldn't fathom at that time how anyone could be sure of anything. I preferred to be banished to my bedroom than to utter a phrase that contained a fixed belief on anything, including what I wanted for dessert.

Given that language is our primary tool for thinking, can we perceive or describe something without first having a linguistic boundary for it? And where does nuance fit in? What about ambiguity? The French philosopher Jacques Derrida stated that we inhabit "a world of signs without fault, without truth, and without origin." One of the central tenets of his philosophy is that "there is nothing outside the text." Derrida's philosophy is named deconstruction, an apt name, since its adherents seek to deconstruct the nature and meaning of language. Several phrases expressing this point of view—intentionally or unintentionally—have floated into our cultural discourse. Two of them are: "We really can't know if something is true or not," a maxim of the deconstructionists, and Bill Clinton's infamous equivocation, "That depends on what the meaning of *is* is."

Critics of Derrida complain that if words have no essential meaning, then there is no meaning. Or, if there is meaning, you can't actually communicate it. I fundamentally disagree.

Design is first and foremost a language that is dependent upon words in order to communicate meaning.

Symbols and actions have as much profundity as words. In fact, facial gestures are all but universal and far more trustworthy when it comes to reading a situation than language can be.

Nevertheless language can be helpful. Back in Tokyo, while hiring a taxi to transport me from the middle of Tokyo back to my hotel, I found that the elderly taxi driver had no idea what I was saying and where I was asking him to go. As my attempts to communicate proved fruitless, I began to ask passersby if they could assist me. A young Japanese woman came over, and I asked her if she could help me tell the cab driver where I was going, as I was lost. It seemed that she understood the word "lost," and I began to feel relieved. But before I knew it, she got into the cab alongside me and started feeling around the floor! She falteringly asked me, "What lost?" Before I could answer, she motioned to other passersby.

Suddenly five generous people began looking for something I hadn't lost in (and around) the taxi.

I couldn't help but laugh and consider the various things one actually could lose: your confidence, your control, your appetite, your dignity, your reputation, your keys, your dog, your faith, your shirt, your heart, your mind, your life. I had simply lost my way. It took a few minutes, but I was finally able to correct the miscommunication by showing the growing group a postcard of the hotel at which I was staying, which I fortuitously remembered was in my handbag. The image did the trick, and then all of us—the young woman, the elderly cab driver, the burgeoning crowd of helpers and me—burst into spontaneous clapping and laughter. Not a word was uttered, not a phrase was exchanged, but suddenly, everyone was on exactly the same page, and all was understood.

Debbie Millman is president of the design division at Sterling Brands. She has been there for 18 years and in that time she has worked on the redesign of over 200 global brands, including projects with P&G, Colgate, Nestle, Kraft and Pepsi.

Debbie is president emeritus of AIGA, the largest professional association for design in the world. She is a contributing editor at *Print* magazine and co-founder and chair of the world's first Masters in Branding Program at the School of Visual Arts in New York City. In 2005, she began hosting, "*Design Matters*," the first podcast about design on the Internet. In 2011, the show was awarded a Cooper Hewitt National Design Award.5

She is the author of five books on design and branding, including the best-selling *Brand Thinking and Other Noble Pursuits*. Last year, an exhibition of her visual essays debuted at the Chicago Design Museum.

Not so stuck in Iceland

by Andrew Johnstone

The day started well. I had been in Iceland for just under a week and was thoroughly enjoying myself. This was my first trip there and I had already grown a deep appreciation for the country.

It was one of the most unique and visually beautiful places I had ever been, and I was getting some great photos of the landscape as I drove through the south past waterfalls, glaciers, mountains and stunning coastline. The previous day had been one of the most spectacular drives of my life through a rugged coastal area that kept getting more beautiful the further east I drove.

Refreshed and ready to see some more of Iceland's beauty, I awoke that morning in a small town called Breidhdalsvik. After a quick breakfast I jumped in the Jeep rental and headed north on what appeared to be a lovely day. The weather in Iceland can change quite dramatically within minutes. This was mid-June, the start of summer, but it was still quite cold, at least for me, an Australian. On this day, though, it was sunny with only scattered clouds.

The start of the drive was relaxing, as I wound up a long and isolated valley with mountains on each side. As is normal in the southeast of Iceland I had not seen another car in the forty minutes or so I had been driving. As I climbed up the head of the valley I looked back and was astounded by the view. While such picturesque views had become the norm over the last few days, this particular valley stood out as one of the most impressive. I pulled over and left the car running while I snapped a few photos. The view was stunning and I snapped off around ten photos and then stopped briefly to enjoy what I was seeing.

It was then that things took a bad turn. Turning away from the view, I tried to open the passenger door to place my camera inside. It was locked. *Not to worry*, I thought, *most likely the driver door will still be unlocked*. It wasn't. It was then that I had that sinking feeling. I tried all the doors and they were all locked. My mobile phone, jacket, wallet and basically everything else was locked in the car, engine still running. I was in an isolated valley wearing a shirt and jeans in around 12 degrees Celsius [approximately 54 ° F]. The sun was out and I was warm enough, but clouds were starting to build and I could feel the temperature dropping even as I had been shooting photos.

I'm quite proud to say that I didn't panic. Being a city guy, this kind of thing had never happened to me before. Adventure enthusiasts or country folk may be laughing to themselves and thinking that this was not a reason to panic.

But as a designer whose biggest concern was usually what weight of Helvetica to use, I felt some apprehension.

As I stood to the side of the car wondering what to do, I noticed a set of headlights winding up the valley. I gave them a wave as they approached and out popped three Austrian's, one of whom was living in Iceland. They were very helpful and sympathetic to my predicament, letting me use their mobile phone to call an emergency number that I had noticed on road signs over the last few days. They explained that they'd get someone to come let me in soon. *Great I thought*, relieved that it shouldn't take too long. The Austrians asked if I wanted a lift but given that all my gear was in the car I declined and they set off.

An hour and a half or so later, the temperature was starting to drop, the clouds were getting thicker and I was increasingly uncomfortable. I lay across the hood of the car using the warmth of the still running engine to help keep from getting too cold. No cars had passed in over an hour, and I was starting to get a little concerned that these emergency people might never arrive.

Finally I noticed another car approaching up the valley and flagged them down. It turned out to be two German ladies who were traveling around Iceland. Their English was limited but they quickly understood my problem and let me use their phone. The emergency people said it could take another few hours, not showing much sympathy to the fact that I was stuck outside without any real protection from the elements, possibly not so unusual an occurrence in Iceland. Unsure what to do I called the car rental company, who also did not show much sympathy but suggested that, if no other option could be found, I break one of the windows.

The strangest thing about this interaction was the realization that breaking the window had never occurred to me, at least not yet. Once voiced it seemed obvious. Of course I should just break the window. Of course! Later, in the comfort and warmth of my hotel room I realized that one of the main reasons for this was how much value we put on cars. I had spent a good portion of my life trying my best not to harm cars, so the idea that I should damage one deliberately did not come easily.

Breaking the window itself did not come easily either.

You know in movies how they smash them with their fist or some poor fool's head? Well, in modern cars at least, that doesn't happen.

Unbeknownst to me the main side windows of most modern cars are more plastic than glass so they do not shatter in an accident. Very smart, but this caused my first few attempts, big rock in hand, to bounce off like I was throwing a basketball. One of the German ladies even tried to kick it for me, ending up flat on her bottom and denting the door rather than the window. In other circumstances that would have been hilarious, but not this one.

After a quick call to the rental office again, feeling very, very stupid, they said to try the hatch windows at the back. This was an

SUV so it had small windows looking into the boot. After a quick check, I saw that they were glass. Just one well-aimed bang with the rock smashed the side window and with some help from the ladies and a bit of wriggling over shattered glass I was back in the car. Hallelujah!

Again, this was never an overly dangerous situation. The Discovery Channel isn't going to be interested in re-creating my epic hardship. But I still learned a few things that day: (1) that I was pretty useless in an emergency; (2) that you should always take the keys and your mobile with you, even if you only travel a few meters from the car; (3) that you should check the consistency of a window before trying to smash it and end up with a two thousand dollar bill to pay; and that German lesbians are often helpful, but a little surly.

Andrew Johnstone is the founder of Design is Kinky, one of the original design community websites. He also cofounded the Semi-Permanent creative events, a series of inspirational worldwide gatherings. In his rare spare time he publishes two magazines. An art magazine called *Empty* and a photography magazine called *Take*. He lives and works in Sydney, Australia.

Fourty-four

by Chris Heimbuch

I turn forty-four this year. My father died when he was forty-four. This year is the forty-fourth anniversary of the Stonewall Riots in Manhattan's Greenwich Village, where I grew up. It's all relative.

My father, Paul Heimbuch, the second oldest of six children, was raised during the 1950s in a middle-class, Irish Catholic family. He grew up across the river from New York City in the town of Weehawken, New Jersey, famous for Hess Oil and its postcard-perfect views of the city skyline.

A funny, intelligent man and talented artist who loved the theater, my father was in the first wave of patients diagnosed with AIDS in the early 1980s. After a brief illness, he died in the spring of 1985: forty-four years old.

This is the story of how a family that struggled with my father's sexuality and illness came together and experienced a healing through the collaborative process of making a quilt in his name. To honor a life too short.

Completed ten years after his death, the quilt I initiated on behalf of my father, now travels the world as a part of *The Names Project* and portrays the story of his life, as told by his friends and family. His quilt, which measures 3' × 6', is part of the larger tapestry, woven into the story of a generation, perhaps two, lost in the tsunami that was the initial onslaught of AIDS.

I was in the backseat of my grandmother's Cadillac when my world and childhood changed forever. My mother sat in the front seat, on the passenger side. Both of us waited for my grandmother to return from a hair appointment she had at the mall. I was fourteen, about to be fifteen, too young to drive; my mother, originally from Michigan but now a full-fledged New Yorker, was without a driver's license. And so we waited together. Parked in a back lot.

My mother's side of the family, also Irish-Catholic, consisted of lots of kids and constant activity. In the midst of a busy time in my life—I stayed on my uncle's farm in Michigan for the summer—this day was a rare, quiet afternoon. It was in the fleeting serenity of this moment that my mother chose to tell me, in a hushed, gentle voice, "Chris, your dad is very sick." A pause, followed by a deep breath. "He has cancer."

My parents had divorced several years earlier, but in the weeks that he had become sick and in the months that followed they would become close friends again. This friendship and tenderness not only benefit-ted my father during his illness, but his family would benefit from my mother's reemergence into their lives as well—long past his death.

The image of my father sick slowly sinking in, I turned my head away from her voice and stared out at the half-filled parking lot, my chest heavy with the weight of this news. A lump in my throat began to throb. I knew it wasn't cancer. I knew he had AIDS.

In adolescent defense of preventing further discussion around the topic, I responded with the most earnest reply I could, telling her it must be the years he spent smoking cigarettes that caused his ill-ness. Another pause and deep breath followed. "I don't think so, hon," she said. Sensing I now needed space, she shifted toward the front of the car and looked out the window, gazing no place in particular. We waited in silence for my grandmother to return. I pretended to fall asleep on the backseat.

The normal routine for kids like me with divorced parents was to visit your father on weekends. On Saturday mornings I would walk from my mother's apartment in the West Village, to my father's apart-ment in the Chelsea district of Manhattan. It was a twenty-minute walk. Hip and cool now, Chelsea was a rougher community back in the day, featuring a cross of black, Latino and white lower-middle class folks. Great music was always in the air and someone's mother or aunt or older sister was perpetually on a stoop looking out for everyone regardless of their background. This was the innocence of the time on West 20th Street.

Large parts of our Saturdays together were spent in my father's design studio. He was an art director, a job and title I would hold myself soon after college. While he'd work, I would happily sketch away for hours or create my own versions of clients with the endless supplies of Letraset type he had in the office. Often lost in our own worlds, side by side in silence, these were cherished afternoons with my father.

Later in the day, we would shop at the farmers market for the evening's dinner. He was a great cook, and I vividly recall the stuffed green peppers he would make for the two of us. They were my favor-ite. He would also make some kind of side dish and a salad as well. He loved to cook.

During all of this preparation, if I was reading in the other room or simply ignoring my chores in the kitchen, he would wail away in his own very sarcastic, very silly way, "I'm slaving away over this hot stove with no help. Slaaaving away ... " That always made me laugh.

Saturday night was for watching television. We would watch *Name That Tune*, *The Love Boat* and *Fantasy Island,* one after the other. Like any goofy dad (or anyone who has ever watched *Fantasy Is-land* for that matter) my father, without fail or hesitation, could never resist saying "Da plane! Da plane!" He, as I do now, wore a joke out. A history shared due to shared DNA.

But before we settled in for ABC prime time, we would first watch the evening news together. This was around 1984, and I still wonder if we watched the news as part of our weekend routine or if my father was really watching it to hear if any progress was being made on the mysterious autoimmune disease sweeping the country (and the world) and devastating the gay community. When a segment about AIDS would come on, a stillness fell over the room; breaths literally and figuratively held; eyes trained on a 9" Toshiba black-and-white TV in effort to make sense of this emerging nightmare that was unfolding before us, and to him.

In those moments, my entire body froze and went rigid with anxiety. I still remember thinking, *In a few years we'll laugh about this and it will all be over. Dad will be okay.* My adolescent defense tried to protect me against the deep fear I had about him being sick. About the private truth that he had AIDS. About the thoughts I had of his not making it. No one did back.

In the decade that followed my father's death, my family didn't talk much about him. Silence, indeed, equaled death.

The risk was far too great for any of us to bring up his name in conversation. Remembering Paul would be to acknowledge that he was gone, and that his life had been taken by AIDS, which he acquired because and only because he was gay. The rare times his name would come up, however, were quickly followed by another topic to distract us all. And if the television was on at a relative's house and a story happened to be about AIDS, the channel was immediately changed, or worse, the television was turned off.

Once a central figure in the family due to his sweet, soft-spoken nature, his holiday cooking and ability to make everyone laugh, my father's forty-four-year history was reduced to a few lines every so often.

This was an extremely difficult time and I was very angry for many years and about many things. I was still dealing with his loss, but I was also dealing with what felt like the denial of my father's life, due to the absence in which we would discuss him. That pain ran very deep, and I needed to do something about it. What I did next probably saved my life from depression and the desperate sense of isolation I found myself gravitating towards.

Awareness around the Internet in 1994 was building, but e-mail was far from ubiquitous and cell phones were still a luxury. Letters and landlines were still the principal methods of communication. For the project I was about to undertake I would use them both. A lot and often.

It started with a letter I sent to my father's siblings and close friends. In it, I addressed that we were approaching the ten-year anniversary of my father's absence from our physical lives and that I wanted to do something to acknowledge this moment. I also wanted to acknowledge that it was AIDS that took his life ten years earlier. Finding my courage, I further shared that I wanted to make a quilt for him together, as a family. And last, that I wanted to have a mass for him, during which we would honor his history and relationship to us. A gay man who died of AIDS, yes, but also, a father, a son, an uncle, a husband, a friend and an artist.

I followed that letter with phone calls and, for the first time, I was speaking openly with my aunts, uncles and my father's friends, about my father having died of AIDS. Some conversations were difficult, some very easy. For the most part, though, none of those first calls were easy at all. For anyone. They were equal parts daunting and elating. Each one was cathartic.

Some people were concerned with who would be involved in this family event. One concern in particular was that some of my younger cousins had not been told the truth about my father and why he actually died. Let alone that their uncle was gay. My cousins at the time of his death were too young and wouldn't have understood. Discussing the complexities of his sexuality also would have been difficult. Now that I am much older, though still not a parent myself, I understand the instinct and need to protect those young lives from something no one truly understood in full—at the time.

My grandmother was in her seventies at the time that I wrote the letter and though my father had been gone nearly ten years, she and I rarely spoke of him. It was killing us both. Rounding out all these conversations (principally with his siblings) the question was repeatedly asked: "Are you planning on talking to Grandma?" And naturally, I was. Of course, I was. This was about healing. About his peace. We would have neither, let alone *he*, my father would have no true peace without the participation of his own mother.

On a rainy Saturday afternoon, an hour and a half from the city, my mother joined me for one of the biggest moments of my life. She was there for moral support, as she has been for much of my life, and was the rock that I would need (as she had been throughout all of this) as I shared my plans (and dreams) with my grandmother in her kitchen later that day.

I took New Jersey Transit from Penn Station down to the Jersey Shore; my grandmother resided in West Long Branch, New Jersey, at the time.

We arrived at Grandma's and settled in, had some laughs as we always did and around lunchtime, she put out a spread of cold cuts on white bread with yellow mustard. Entenmann's chocolate cake was offered in plenty. Any other day, this would be a great summer afternoon. But there was tension in the air and my grandmother knew this was no ordinary visit from the city for me. Nerves were palpable. The air was heavy. As my mother did years earlier: a pause, followed by a deep breath. Then, internal calm.

Looking my grandmother in her beautiful Irish eyes, I came out for my father. I told her that her oldest son had been gay and, in the most gentile way I could, that he had died of AIDS. My hands in hers, clenching tighter and tighter, she had questions. We talked. She had more questions and we talked some more. And then, it was all ... okay. A mother knows.

It took some time for her to understand what the quilt we were making for my father was, but more importantly after understanding— and understanding why I had to do this—my grandmother said she wanted to participate and that, of course, she would attend his mass.

Relieved and exhausted, I went to the living room to breathe again. Searching the radio station for Frank Sinatra, to my awe, Bruce Springsteen's "Philadelphia" came on. My mother and I looked at one another from across the room. With chills running through us both, words were not spoken; they were unnecessary. From that moment on, we knew everything was going to be all right. For my grandmother, for the family. For my father.

We had the mass the following spring in the West Village at Saint Joseph's Church. Through all the horror of the eighties, when it felt that everyone in the community was losing a friend, a lover or a father, Saint Joseph's was a beacon of hope. Of more profound importance, it

" "

Looking my grandmother in her beautiful Irish eyes, I came out for my father.

" "

was a Church of acceptance. It is for this reason that we were blessed to work with a most incredible pastor, Father Aldo Tos. He helped to bring closure, proper, peaceful and loving closure, to my father's life. Forever grateful to him, I shall be.

In the foyer and entrance of Saint Joseph's, prominently displayed to greet all those who attended, was my father's quilt. His mother, siblings, nephews, nieces, friends and his greatest caretaker in his last days—my mother—joined, witnessed and participated in our final goodbye to him. With love and understanding. With tears and hugs. He was no longer someone we were afraid to talk about. We acknowledged the complete man he was and the lives he touched. Mainly, we honored a life now lost.

Years later, one of my father's sisters and his biggest protector growing up would work with AIDS patients in Alabama. The daughter of another aunt would later become a Director at the Gay Men's Heath Organization in NYC. As a family, we talk regularly about my father with no fear of anything at all. We merely remember a man who died way too young. We remember his laughter and remember him. There are no more secrets.

New life is being born into this family this year. I have two beautiful cousins pregnant with their first children. Life goes on.

I turn forty-four this year. The same age my father was when he died. I think how fast my life has gone, poignantly marked this year now that we share the same age. What's gone even faster are the nearly thirty years since he died.

Memory serves to remind me that some of my most special times with my father were in his studio, creating art, side by side. And the creation of the quilt, undoubtedly artwork in its own right, serves as tangible evidence of the love for my father. I create art to this day, and he is never far from my mind.

My solace and peace is the quilt that shares his story with the world. Because of *The Names Project*, his story is shared with people who are strangers to me, strangers that I love and support due to the common bond that weaves our stories together. I hope when others see his story on our quilt, they understand a family created it together for someone they loved very much. I hope that brings them strength and courage. I hope it brings them peace, as it did for me. As it did for Paul Heimbuch.

A father, a son, an uncle, a husband, a friend and an artist.

A native New Yorker, Chris Heimbuch was born and raised in Greenwich Village. He holds a BFA in Design and has been working in design and technology for the past 20 years. Now living in San Francisco, Chris is currently the director of brand operations for Square.

Six weeks with no shoes

by Josh Higgins

Before I begin, let me give you a little context to this story. Starting in middle school, I played in several bands over the years, but in 1994 the band I was playing in, fluf, signed with MCA/Universal Records and everything changed.

We received an endorsement deal with Fender Musical Instruments so now basses, strings and amps were free, and there's nothing better than that for a musician. We started touring a lot more. We went from an eighteen-passenger van we drove ourselves to a bus with a driver. We toured with some of my all-time favorite bands: Jawbreaker, Jimmy Eat World, Face to Face, Rocket From The Crypt, Bad Religion, Rancid, Fugazi and the list goes on. We were one of a dozen bands to play the first ever Warped Tour. (Side note: No Doubt was one of the "special guests" opening the shows that first tour. Now I'm showing my age.)

The second Warped Tour was in 1996. The lineup that year was, Fishbone, Pennywise, CIV, Dance Hall Crashers, Down by Law, Deftones, Sense Field, Far, NOFX and the Might Mighty Bosstones. It was shaping up to be a great tour. On the itinerary was Denver's Red Rocks Amphitheatre, a venue I had always wanted to play. Our friends from San Diego, Rocket From The Crypt and Blink-182, were also on the tour so we knew some other bands already. The thing about the Warp Tour is, even if you know no one at the start of the tour, by the end you know everyone and some lifelong friendships are forged. A lot of high jinks went on during the tour: water balloons hitting you while doing a sound check, another band sneaking onto your bus and planting sandwiches in your bunk. You get the idea. On days off, of which there were not many (maybe one day off every two weeks), the production team would schedule outings for bands that wanted to do something different. For instance, some bands went skydiving or river rafting, and I recall one day we took over a water park near the show's venue.

On one day off when we were in Oregon, the production team put together a three-hour rafting trip down the Rogue River. It was mayhem. Everyone was trying to capsize each other, grabbing the oars out of each other's hands and throwing them so there was no way to navigate. But then, during a mellow part of the river, things settled down and became pretty calm.

When you float down a river, after a while people naturally separate from each other because of the current. During that time I fell asleep. I was laid back in the raft with my legs over the side. At the end of the float, some people near me noticed I was asleep and thought a good way to alert me the trip was about to end was to nudge my raft into a metal dingy that was docked. It made a very loud noise when I hit it, and that did a great job of waking me up. I immediately jumped out of the raft so as not to miss the stopping point, and as I did, I realized that my legs had fallen asleep. When I hit the floor of the river, my legs immediately went out and I went under.

The people that put me into the dingy laughed, as did all of the people on the shore who happened to be watching. I went back to our bus to shower and then jumped in my bunk for a nap before dinner. When I woke up, I noticed my feet were still numb.

I looked down and they were the size of two altered tomatoes with one large blister covering the entire top of each foot. *Damn it, what a idiot!* I thought. I had forgot to put sunscreen on my feet.

The next day I had a nurse look at my feet, and she said I had second-degree burns on them. They were so swollen, I was not able to wear shoes for the next six weeks! Every day I played barefoot. Shows that we played in daylight, I tried to maneuver around my side of the stage so sunlight did not touch my feet because if it did, it burned like they were on fire. So there I was a week later, playing a sold-out show at Red Rocks barefoot, hobbling around the stage trying to avoid sunlight. My feet became a topic of conversation for the rest the tour.

I had always wanted to meet Angelo from Fishbone. When I finally did, the first thing he said to me was, "Hey, you're the guy with the sunburned feet. That sucks."

To this day musicians from that tour, roadies, catering people, you name it, remember my sunburned feet. Just recently, I saw Mark from Blink-182, and he said, "Remember your feet?"

So my advice to all is, when applying sunscreen, don't forget your feet.

....

Josh Higgins is a creative who works across multiple mediums including digital, print, apparel, packaging, identity, broadcast, and environmental design creating consistent experiences between brands and consumers. For over thirteen years, he's been refining the art of connecting brands to people with a concept-driven visual style that has earned him national honors.

Currently comanaging the communication design team at Facebook, Josh recently concluded his role as design director for President Obama's 2012 campaign. As the design director, Josh built and led the design team for the historic 2012 political campaign in which the web, design, and technology played a pivotal role. The responsibility of Josh and the team was to design the Obama 2012 campaign both online and offline. A main focus of his was on creating a uniform message and consistent visual language across all mediums.

Josh dedicates a percentage of his time to social causes. Finding creative ways to support them has manifested into successful exhibits and charitable projects like The Hurricane, So-Cal and Haiti Poster Projects, in addition to lecture series with photographers, designers and film makers with proceeds donated to various charitable organizations.

Before they were famous

by Art Chantry

Ted was a semi-mythological bogeyman in the northwest long before we knew who he really was. Even before they caught him, everybody up here in the northwest had a "Ted story."

Seems dang near everyone brushed up against him somewhere, at some time. Although many of the stories I've been told were obviously little more than fantasies, many of them have proven to be true. I know people who still have nightmares about him. I've even known people who had sisters and friends murdered by him. He left an indelible mark on us up here.

Back around 1973, I was living in Tacoma and working as a garbage man for Pacific Lutheran University, where I also attended classes for a time (yes, it's true). Almost every evening I would get together with a drinking buddy and go prowling around Tacoma for something—anything—to do. Out on South Tacoma way—right next to the old location of the UPS (University of Puget Sound) law school back then—there was a cheesy student tavern called The Creekwater Dispensary. It was a typical sort of tavern in those days, pre-sports bar and not yet anything we'd call hip or cool. Just a place to drink beer. They had pinball machines (this was before video games) and one single coin-op pool table in the back.

This place was a regular hang-out for me and my friend Bill. We usually started our evening adventures there. The place was never very crowded, and we were pretty good pool players. We could go to the back and challenge the table (coin-op rules). If we won, we could hold the table and play all evening for free and drink beers we won, too (until we got drunk enough to lose). That's why we became so good—it meant free beer. (Yeah, for a very short time in my life I hustled pool for free beer.) However, as good as I got, I was "streaky." I never could quite master bank shots (though I was great at reading "English.") I had even mastered combo shots and jump shots, but I never could exactly read a bank shot. Thank God Bill was usually with me. He was terror on a pool table.

There was one other regular at the bar that I vividly remember. He was usually alone, shooting pool by himself when we showed up. He was a student attending classes at the UPS law school next door and would come around after classes to relax. Boy, this guy really needed relaxing, too. He was one uptight asshole. That's why we *loved* it when he was there. We could *always* beat this guy no matter how badly we played or how good he played. When he was there holding the table, we were happy, because we could make quick work of him and win the table and start getting that free beer. He was easy pickins.

The guy was a little on the short side—maybe 5'8" or so. He always seemed to wear white flared pants (remember this was 1973 or 1974) and a black long-sleeved turtleneck sweater. He was sort of handsome (especially when he smiled, which we only saw him do once or twice). He had this full shock of dark slightly curly hair on his head, medium length. Frankly he was classic collegiate lady-killer looks—what we called "preppie" back then. We, on the other hand, were dirtbag locals. And we played the part well, as Bill had usually just gotten off swing shift at the Atlas Foundry where he worked as a grinder, and I often still reeked of garbage.

So imagine these two dirt bags (us) putting a quarter challenge to the elite law student guy who held the table—an arrogant preppie asshole.

How does this work out? All we had to do was play well—even if it was for a very short run. He would get so *pissed*! And when he got pissed, we always won, because he would choke like mad. In fact, he rarely finished a game because he'd throw his pool cue on the floor and stomp away. *Success!* It worked like charm. We used to even tease him about it. No matter how many times we played him, this was almost always the only result. We *loved* this guy!

Cut to fifteen years later. My girlfriend back then was reading a book on serial killers. I had been entertaining her with my "Tacoma stories" and I had told her about this guy. He was so memorable that I'd actually turned him into an entertaining little anecdote. She began to question me: "What was the name of that tavern you used to shoot pool at all the time in Tacoma?" "About what year was this?" "What time of day?" "Remember that asshole you talked about who you could always beat because he got pissed?" Finally she held up the book that was turned to a full-page photo and said, "Did he look like this?" Wham!

It was a picture of the guy we played pool with! And it was Ted Bundy! No doubt about it, it was him. That photo was the spitting image of that asshole in the tavern. Seems Ted used to hang out there so often that the tavern actually made a book about him—down to the details of when and where and how. So that jerk we used to shoot pool

Man of the decade:
Ted Bundy through the years

1973

1974

1975

1976

1977

1978

1979

Below:
As he appears today

with and constantly piss off was old bogeyman Ted himself! Maybe we should have let him win once in a while. Think of the lives we could have saved ...

Usually my essays have something to do with graphic design in some vague manner—and here comes that part. Back in those days there was a cartoonist who used to hang out at the Creekwater, too. He was always hustling people to buy him a beer and he'd draw them a cartoon caricature of them in exchange (hell, we were *all* broke back then). He did okay. (Anybody out there remember this guy? Is he still around?)

That cartoonist managed to talk the owner into doing an exchange—free beer for doing a mural in the back on the blank wall above the pool table. He worked on that for a long, long time and nursed a *lot* of free beer the whole while. What he painted on that wall was a huge group of cartoon caricatures (sorta like those guys who will draw a quick cartoon of you and your honey when you visit the carnival or the Pike Street Market). He did caricature portraits of all the bar regulars—dozens of them. I was in there, my friend Bill was in there. And also TED was in there!

I was actually painted into a mural alongside Ted Bundy!

That old tavern is now a Korean restaurant. The UPS law school moved away decades ago. Ted is very, very dead (thank god). That mural on that wall has been painted over god knows how many times. But underneath all those layers of paint, there actually exists a mural of me and Bill and Ted Bundy, the happy campers. Pool, anyone?

Raised in Tacoma, Art Chantry worked in Seattle for nearly 30 years. During that time he managed to produce a body of work that, however unorthodox, still rivals some of the best graphic design in the world. He has won hundreds of design and advertising awards, including a bronze lion at Cannes, and the Poster Laureate of the Colorado International Invitational Poster Exposition. His work has been collected and exhibited by some of the most prestigious museums and galleries in the world: the Louvre, The Smithsonian, The Library of Congress and the Rock and Roll Hall of Fame to name a few. In 1993, The Seattle Art Museum honored him with a one-man retrospective of his work. PS1, in association with the Museum of Modern Art, did the same. His work has been published in hundreds of books and magazines and Chronicle Books published the monograph of his work, *Some People Can't Surf,* written by Julie Lasky. In fact, there is even a book about Chantry's work published in China and written entirely in Chinese … though nobody knows what it really says.

During his time working in Seattle, Art somehow managed to carve out a style that took hold of the popular underground music scene in the early 1990s. Dubbed "grunge" by culture mavens, it actually was a look developed at an alternative newsweekly named *The Rocket*, where Art began as art director in 1984 and continued to be involved off and on for over ten years. During that time, the magazine became a virtual hub on the wheel of Seattle's music and culture scene. Soon his ideas extended beyond *The Rocket* to the fledgling record label, Sub Pop, where it became history. His ideas found further nuance in his work for the garage rock record label, Estrus Records, where his style found a perfect home.

Through his work with the staff of *The Rocket* and the classes he taught at the School of Visual Concepts, Art influenced an entire generation of young graphic designers in the northwest, and eventually across the county. He has lectured extensively and traveled to present his work all over the world. He has contributed writings to a number of books about graphic design, and his own book, *Instant Litter: Concert Posters from Seattle Punk Culture*, is considered a classic in its field. To this day, his hardedge scrappy look can be seen everywhere from punk rock record covers to corporate annual reports.

After tea

by John Maeda

I had accepted an invitation from Ikko Tanaka to attend a traditional Japanese tea ceremony at his house in a special tearoom he had designed himself.

It was a normal, absurdly hot and humid summer evening in Tokyo when I entered the room with two other guests. One of them was an up-and-coming architect who

Photo: Jon Kamen

had achieved fame with his humanitarian project for a distressed part of Japan; the other was a famous art director who was notorious for his scandalous photos juxtaposing tastefully positioned type on seminude photographs. My work combining computer code with traditional visual arts thinking was just beginning to get past a protracted, stalled phase and was starting to make more sense.

It was a special evening, though I distinctly recall feeling extremely nervous around the guests assembled there—especially the legendary host. When I was passed the bowl of tea—with its faintly colored ceramic surfaces that had survived in the care of Mr. Tanaka's family for centuries—I held my breath so as to not drop the ancient chalice. The ceremony ended after an hour's time, and I felt transformed by the experience. I left with the hope of giving something of value back to Mr. Tanaka to properly show my appreciation to him.

When I returned to my studio at home, which was two and a half hours from Tokyo, I designed a special package with a hand-lettered card. It took a while to make it, and all the while I kept wondering whether the quality would be worthy of Mr. Tanaka. But my father taught me from a young age that thanking people with sincerity is an activity I should never take lightly. So I went to sleep satisfied that I had done my best and got on the bus the next morning to drop it off at his house. I woke up earlier than usual, got on my bicycle, onto a bus, onto a train and then onto the subway. The evening before I had almost got lost on the way to his house, and I wasn't 100 percent sure I had arrived at the correct house, as the night can play tricks with your mind. But I got up my confidence and slipped it into the slot in the door. Done. And I headed back home.

Indeed, on the surface it seemed a bit impractical to travel five hours to someone's home to drop off a package, but I wanted to show my appreciation somehow.

Weeks passed, and I didn't hear back from Mr. Tanaka. I began to believe that I put the box into the slot of the wrong house. I began wondering if I should try again, but it was getting a bit late to send a proper thanks. At a party in Tokyo, one of our mutual friends said to me how happy Mr. Tanaka was to receive my gift. He told her how the famous Japanese architect had sent flowers to his house, while the young man from America had dropped a package off at his house personally.

Mr. Tanaka commented that, "The American fellow was more Japanese than my Japanese guests," and as a result, he wanted to take me under his wing. I subsequently was invited to participate in a variety of his projects, during which I learned more than I could have imagined about traditional design. Mr. Tanaka's guidance and support truly changed the course of my life.

The moral of my story is that sometimes luck shines your way when you are conscious of your actions and focusing on gratitude as a means of communication rarely does you harm.

John Maeda is a leader who imagines how design can simplify technology and help leaders respond to new challenges in the era of social media. His work as a graphic designer, computer scientist, artist and educator earned him the distinction of being named one of the 75 most influential people of the 21st century by *Esquire*.

In June 2008, Maeda became president of Rhode Island School of Design, and in late 2012, Business Insider named RISD the #1 design school in the world. At RISD, Maeda is leading the movement to transform STEM (Science, Technology, Engineering and Math) to STEAM by adding art. Called the "Steve Jobs of academia" by *Forbes*, he believes art and design are poised to transform our economy in the 21st century like science and technology did in the last century.

Maeda previously served as associate director of research at the MIT Media Lab. He serves on the boards of Sonos, Quirky, and Wieden+Kennedy, and on the Davos World Economic Forum's Global Agenda Council on New Models of Leadership. His books include *The Laws of Simplicity*, *Creative Code*, and *Redesigning Leadership*, which expands on his Twitter feed at @johnmaeda, one of *TIME Magazine's* 140 Best Twitter Feeds of 2012. Maeda received the AIGA Medal in 2010 and is in the permanent collection of the Museum of Modern Art.

The driving test

by Alissa Walker

Did you have senior superlatives at your high school?

It would appear that most schools have abolished this concept in today's educational climate, since cyberbullying on Facebook has proved to be so much more convenient.

In the early 1990s, at Parkway West Senior High School in Chesterfield, Missouri, we were still doling out ballots to our fellow classmates, conducting a search for winning candidates in areas of achievements like Best Looking, Best Dressed and Best All-Around.

You didn't campaign for senior superlatives, but the chatter in the locker bay served as a kind of an ongoing Situation Room. For some categories, the pundits agreed, there were clear front-runners. As we edged toward election day, the conventional wisdom had determined that I would be named not one of the best, but one of the worst. When the results were tallied later that week it became official: I was voted Worst Driver by my senior high school class.

My worst driver male counterpart was Mike Wheeler. He had earned this distinction by totaling a car. To add to the poetic bliss, Mike Wheeler brought his dismembered steering wheel to school for the photo shoot. I didn't have any physical proof of my bad driving, so I simply held up my car keys. And there we were, a Walker and a Wheeler, immortalized in the yearbook as the school's worst drivers. Class of 1995, 4-EVA.

I had not totaled a car. I had not maimed a pedestrian. I believe, at the time, I had only gotten one speeding ticket for going 10 mph over the speed limit on a quiet residential street. Yet my short driving history had transformed me into an urban legend at my school: I failed my driver's test so many times, I almost didn't get my license.

It wasn't that I was a bad driver. Rather I would call myself an indifferent one. When I first climbed behind the wheel under the supervision of my parents, as Missouri law allows one to do at the age of fifteen, the transition from the passenger seat to the driver's seat felt like a demotion. The car was a place where I could play music, survey the landscape, read my Sweet Valley High books. Driving that car meant getting distracted, making mistakes, being yelled at by angry people, many of whom were sitting in the very same vehicle as me.

Driving was annoying.

But being *able* to drive was something else. I was one of the youngest people in my grade so I didn't turn sixteen until my junior year. There were people in my grade who were over a year older than me, who were now professionally driving to parties and football games and the parking lot of McDonald's. Sometimes there'd be an empty middle backseat I could talk my way into, but most of the time I was at home, having failed to procure a ride.

By the time I turned sixteen, I had been left behind.

On September 3, 1993, I was so sure that a laminated plastic rectangle would be mine that when I got behind the wheel with the road-test examiner I was already planning my first parent-free destination (TCBY for a chocolate vanilla swirl). I pulled left out into a busy street like a pro, stopped at the light, then turned right down a residential street as directed.

The examiner, Officer Storey—a name I will never, ever forget— told me to turn right at the next street, and then right again ... right back into the parking lot of the DMV. I smiled, knowing that I had demonstrated such skill in those few blocks that he decided the rest of the test was clearly not necessary. After he instructed me to park the car and turn off the engine, he humorlessly explained that I had automatically failed because I had broken the law.

Wait. "I broke the law?"

He had to explain, in detail, what I did. I had turned right during a red light at an intersection marked no-right-on-red. It was possibly the shortest driving test in Missouri state history.

He did not give me a ticket, although he said that he could have.

I was almost certain this intersection had been staged just for drivers tests, I told my parents. I had never encountered this mythical sign during my short driving career in suburban St. Louis, had they? We decided I had been tricked. I was so convinced my first test was a fluke, I confidently went back the next week.

I knew something was wrong when the examiner (a woman this time) kept writing things down. Not just checking things off, but writing down words. So I started getting nervous.

Which way should the wheels face when you're parking on an uphill street? I guessed.

The pole they have behind the spot in the parallel parking test? Yeah, I hit that.

I had failed for the second time.

I had aced the written test because I was good at memorizing facts. I was failing my road tests because I didn't actually know anything about driving. And, honestly, I didn't want to.

But I had to get that license.

On the first night after I had failed my test, my dad took me car shopping. I thought it was my parents' idea of a cruel joke, since those

"

The pole they have behind the spot in the parallel parking test? Yeah, I hit that.

"

were administered as regularly as dinner in my family. I sat in various early 1990s models in the used car lot, as directed by the salesman who did not know about my license-free status. Above me, metallic streamers glittered across the late summer sky and winged insects darted between them in the blue fluorescent light. I climbed into driver's seat after driver's seat, closing the thick plastic exoskeletons around me, glossy shells that would inevitably become dimpled and bruised on every car I owned.

Like the sixteen-year-olds I had seen in car commercials, I tried my hardest to get excited about the CD player, the snap of the turn signal. But this whole thing—shiny, artificial, complicated—just wasn't me.

When I got home, where I planned to watch *Saturday Night Live* reruns in quiet shame, I threw open the door to the basement stairs, revealing two balloons hovering on the landing. My friends—licensed drivers, all of them—were there for a surprise party my parents had organized weeks before, when they believed their daughter was capable of reading a no right turn on red sign.

I laughed at my own misfortune as I opened gift bags from my friends containing various scented lotions from The Body Shop. And one by one, they left, in their Honda Civics and Chrysler LeBarons, which had been carefully parked in the other cul-de-sac so as to not ruin the surprise.

My boyfriend drove me to the McDonald's, where I heard someone's conversation echo across the parking lot, over the chatter of the drive-thru speaker.

"Dude, that's the chick who failed her driver's test."

"No way."

Determined to save face, I drank a beer, and then another one, and then another one, out of a cooler in the trunk of a Mitsubishi Eclipse. I drank them so quickly that when my boyfriend took me home, I was clumsy letting myself into the garage, and my parents later told me that they immediately knew I had been drinking. In my self-sabotaging state I reasoned that I was still license-less, so I might as well be grounded.

Three weeks after my sixteenth birthday, I was back at the DMV, a pool of sweat accumulating below me in a molded plastic seat. The gravity of the situation weighed upon me. If I failed this one, I would have to petition the state to permit me a license.

"Alissa Walker?"

It was Officer Storey.

If he recognized me, he didn't let on. He was cool, just the way you would be if you were holding the fate of a young woman in your hands.

This is the part of the movie where I ace the test, where instead of parking at the DMV I do a victory lap around the strip mall parking lot, high-fiving people piloting grocery carts out of Schnucks, the friendliest store in town.

But the reality was that the third test was every bit as bad as the two that came before.

We pulled back into the parking lot of the DMV, parking in the exact same parking spot where my sentence had been delivered twice before. I looked down at the steering wheel deciding when and how it would be appropriate for me to kiss it goodbye.

"One more failed test and you have to talk to the governor's office."

So he did remember me!

"Well, I'm sorry to have to tell you this." A dramatic pause lasting five license-less lifetimes settled into the center console between us. "But you passed."

Oh, now he had a sense of humor.

He handed over the test sheet. It was true that I passed.

It was also true that I had only passed by a handful of points.

Anyone could see the relief in my face in my driver's license photo. I had won.

But I had lost. I had been forced, against my will, into a driving career. Because I saw no other options in my suburban St. Louis life, I climbed inside this alien creature that would come to define me, displace me and disgrace me for the next decade.

Now I live in L.A. On a trip back home a few years ago, I noticed that the McDonald's parking lot where you once could find Natural Lights on ice in the trunk of a Mitsubishi Eclipse and every single one of my friends on a Friday night was only one mile from my house. A twenty-minute walk.

But I never would have made it without my car. In my town, there were no sidewalks.

Lamb wars

by Theresa Neil

Before I became a designer, I worked as a chef. Many of my friends to this day are from the restaurant industry, including my husband.

One day, my craziest chef friend, Monica Cobb, calls with an offer I can't refuse: She wants my husband and me to cater a wedding in the south of France. One twist: neither of us spoke any French.

We pack our bags and head to Europe for the first time, careful to put the knives in our checked bags so we won't get held up in security. Monica picks us up from the airport driving like a madwoman around the steeps curves of the countryside. She's giving us a rundown on the living quarters. We're staying with the wedding party at a villa near Antibes. As we get closer, we see this gorgeous villa and fluffy white sheep dotting the hillside in the distance. "Those are what we're serving," she said, "Did you bring your knives?"

After a couple of glasses of wine, she admits we do not have to butcher an entire flock of sheep; the lamb for the wedding is being delivered. But she does want me to run to the store and pick up the ingredients we'll need to prep the next day. The wedding is the day after, but it will take three days to prep all the food for a five-course meal for one hundred guests.

At the store we encounter only a few translation problems. The main one revolves around my need for fresh, not frozen shrimp, a very difficult thing to communicate. I think my interpretive dance will be remembered fondly by all the fishmongers who witnessed it.

Back at the villa we unpack the supplies and settle in for a tasty dinner of grilled sardines and lively conversation with people from around the globe. I start to relax, this is going to be great, and it hardly even matters that we don't speak the language.

In the morning, I wake up fresh as a daisy, even after drinking three bottles of wine the night before. "I love this country," I tell everyone. "I don't even have a hangover."

We prep all day. Sauces, dressings, marinade for the lamb, all the vegetables for roasting the next day. That evening Monica turns in early, a prudent choice in retrospect. But I stay up to share stories and drink the "no hangover" wine. The villa is overflowing, with gypsies pitching tents on the lawn and at least a dozen people bunked in each room.

At 6 A.M., I crawl into the bed we're all sharing and crawl back out an hour later. I know Monica is going to be up shortly and want to get started for the *big day*. My eyes are bloodshot and hands are shaking, but no hangover yet. However, the jet lag is definitely causing some havoc.

In this "prime" condition, I decide to burrow into a deep stack of chaise lounge cushions that are stored on the balcony. This is where Monica finds me and drags me out by my ear to follow her to the store for the last items on the shopping list.

We hop in the car and go to these adorable outdoor shops, brimming with fresh produce, cured meats and local flowers that are just gorgeous. I find the most remote section of the parking lot to discreetly hurl.

Racing back to the house, I make Monica pull over so I can mark another picturesque spot, this time a field full of wild flowers.

By the time we're back at the villa, I am bent in two, dying. The only thing keeping me upright is Monica's searing anger and knife pointed at me. I bravely continue prepping, but I am working at quarter speed, if that.

Around noon, the butcher shows up with a tiny refrigerated truck of lamb, but we have to turn him away because we have nowhere to store it. There is only one refrigerator in the house, plus a narrow wine fridge, and they are both packed. We make the butcher swear that he will be back with the lamb by 6 P.M. so we can prepare it for the main course. But we're uneasy that something may have been lost in translation.

The stress is escalating. We're working in a tiny space and people keep wandering through and sampling the food we're furiously prepping or accidentally knocking items on the floor. We realize we are desperately short on tomatoes for the ragú so I dash off to buy 20 pounds but return with 20 kilos, more than twice as much as we need. We stack the surplus tomatoes out by the tents the gypsies have pitched and just keep prepping.

While Monica and I deal with the food, our husbands set up the tables and chairs on the hilltop. The surroundings couldn't be more beautiful for a wedding, and we planned a menu to match. The courses will all be served family style on large platters carried out to the tables. We will serve shrimp ragu, roasted asparagus, grilled lamb with mint pesto and fennel, mixed greens with ripe figs, rich stinky French cheese and crunchy prosciutto. Yum.

As six o'clock rolls around, there's no sign of the lamb, but we manage to lock the asparagus in the oven on auto clean, which quickly brings the oven's temp up to about 700° F.

We can't interrupt the wedding party to find a French speaker to translate the oven manual, and I am contemplating breaking the glass to save the asparagus, when I overhear Monica on the porch. She (100 pounds soaking wet) has our native French grill guy, Victor (300 pounds, if an ounce), by the coat, and is miming a throat slashing if his butcher friend doesn't show up with the lamb now.

Thirty minutes later, the tiny reefer truck putters up the side of the hill, and all of the guests cheer. I almost cry in relief, but instead crank up the grill and get down to business.

We served the last slice of cake at midnight and toasted our success. Compliments were thick, as the guests were impressed two Texas girls could pull off French provincial cuisine with flair. As we slumped, exhausted, into our seats, sipping champagne, we looked past all the happy guests to the rows of tables and chairs and stacks of plates and realized ... we forgot to hire a cleanup crew.

Theresa Neil is an international design expert based in Austin, Texas. She is passionate about making products that look good and work well. Her top selling O'Reilly books, *Designing Web Interfaces*, coauthored with Bill Scott, and the *Mobile Design Pattern Gallery* have helped thousands of IT professionals advance their design skills and create better experiences.

Theresa and her team of experts work closely with clients to define and deliver UX solutions for complex problems. Having led the design for 100+ products since 2001, Theresa knows the magic formula to rapidly designing and releasing successful products.

The greatest job
I ever had

by Roman Mars

For some reason I thought I could drive from Athens, Georgia, to San Francisco, California, with only $100 in my bank account.

This is not possible, and is probably reckless, but after I'd burned all the bridges in that small college town, west was the direction I was heading.

My cousin in Memphis saved me from myself. She and her lesbian partner wanted a baby. If I stayed with them in Memphis for a few weeks, I could earn good money delivering pizzas at the Papa John's she managed in the suburbs of Shelby County, but my real job was ejaculating into a sterile syringe.

Five days a week, I would take breadsticks and pizza pies to soccer moms and shut-ins. Several days a month, I would masturbate in my room, knock on my cousin's bedroom door and hand over "the product" for her to insert into her partner. This continued for five months.

For five months, I masturbated and ate as much pizza as I wanted.

....

I had been training for this job as if it were an Olympic event since the age of twelve. It was, without question, the greatest job I ever had.

....

As is, Papa John's pizza is pretty much inedible. But the workers in the store were creative. We'd take the large pizza dough and roll it out really thin to create a massive Italian-style pie with light sauce and cheese. I'd take slices of pepperoni, add a sprinkle of cheese and place them directly on the pizza screen. Run it halfway through the oven, and you get mighty tasty hors d'oeuvres. I put on ten pounds.

This was way before I had a cell phone, so as I drove around the mid-South highways delivering pizzas with the radio as my companion. The public radio station switched to classical music at night, so I relied on commercial radio. I waited hours for "Karma Police" by Radiohead and "Pepper" by the Butthole Surfers to cycle back into rotation each shift. Those songs saved me, but when they let me down, Art Bell saved me. Art Bell's tinfoil hat explorations into the extraterrestrial and paranormal were either certifiably bonkers or savvy satire. I never figured it out.

No baby resulted. Either chance or a biological anomaly got in the way. I moved on to San Francisco. Years later, my cousin's wife had a minor surgery to fix her fallopian tubes and this time they selected a anonymous donor. They got their baby and then another. I had two myself, several years after that.

My job is certainly more interesting now. Quite possibly it's leading to something more interesting still. But there was something about this time that was special to me. All my life I had been ahead of everyone. I skipped grades. Started college at fifteen. Went straight to graduate school after college. I taught kids older than me. I was always ahead. But grad school didn't take and I became a dropout working at Papa John's in Shelby County. I was not a fantastic employee, but I was responsible and polite. While I was there, my future was murky and nothing I was doing made it clearer. But for once, I was where I was. I was just a guy eating pizza and masturbating for a greater good. And it was great indeed.

....

Roman Mars is the creator of *99% Invisible*, a short radio show about design and architecture. With over 10 million downloads, the *99% Invisible* podcast is one of the most popular and highest rated programs in iTunes. *Fast Company* named Mars one of 100 Most Creative People in 2013. *99% Invisible*'s season 3 crowd funding campaign broke all previous records for a journalism project on Kickstarter.

Don't believe the hype

by Michael Vanderbyl

If there's one thing I've learned as a designer, it's that you should never believe your own PR. There have been at least two incidents that have served to foster this philosophy and help me appreciate the value of humility.

In 2000, I designed the identity for AmericaOne, the St. Francis Yacht Club's challenge for that year's America's Cup trophy. The graphics were, as requested by the client, a radical departure from traditional nautical imagery and themes. The colors were electric green and steel gray, a far cry from the customary red, white and blue. The design featured graphic "shards" on the hull, embracing styles analogous of Formula One auto racing to reflect the spirit of the race.

On the day of the launch, Paul Cayard, AmericaOne helmsman and sailing superstar, gave a speech and introduced me to a spirited crowd. He highlighted my concept as he declared that this was the year he would bring the America's Cup back to the St. Francis Yacht Club. I was beaming as the cloth concealing the hull of the boat fell away, exposing the radical new design. The crowd cheered with approval. As I stood there with my wife and daughter, basking in the moment, a small elderly woman made her way earnestly through the crowd toward me. Dressed head-to-toe in red, white and blue, her chunky acrylic sweater adorned with gold lamé anchors. She smiled as she slipped me a small folded bit of paper. I quietly said thank you and smiled back politely, returning my attention to Paul, who was still in the middle of his speech which extolled the new design and me.

Minutes later, I looked down and opened the folded note to find scrawled in blue ink and unsteady handwriting,

"NO ONE likes the new design"—the words NO ONE were underlined twice and further emphasized by four exclamation points.

To add insult to injury, the note writer had embellished the paper with a drawing of a frowning face. I just smiled. It seemed certain that no amount of PR was going to make a difference.

Earlier in my career I was confronted with the harsh futility of believing in my PR. Many years ago, I created the branding for the new bed and bath division of Esprit. This included not only the identity, packaging and retail environments but also product design. Doug Tompkins, then president of Esprit, hesitantly asked if I would be willing to give a presentation at Macy's in the bed and bath department as part of the launch of this new division. I agreed and arrived at Macy's at the appointed time, where about fifty chairs had been arranged, along with a table set with wine and cheese for a small reception. There was a surprisingly good turnout for the event, and I was feeling a bit of an ego boost as the collection had recently been named by *Time Magazine* as one of its "Ten Best" designs of that year.

I approached the podium and began my talk, my voice echoing throughout the department store. Thinking back, this in and of itself was pretty bizarre, and I wonder if shoppers in other areas of the store were puzzled by the voice ringing out of nowhere. I closed my remarks with observations from my point of view as a disenfranchised modernist and described designing the collection to fulfill a need for the modern home; an enthusiastic round of applause followed. Feeling quite pleased with myself, I asked the audience if there were any questions. There was a pause, just long enough for me to think no one had a questions, when suddenly a hand shot up in the very last row. I was filled with anticipation as I waited to hear what insightful query might be made. A floppy-hat-wearing elderly woman, hands overflowing with refreshments, rose from her seat and asked, "Is there any more cheese?"

Michael Vanderbyl has gained international prominence in the design field as a practitioner, educator, critic and advocate. Since being established in San Francisco in 1973, his firm, Vanderbyl Design, has evolved into a multidisciplinary studio with expertise in identity, print and digital communications, interiors, showrooms, retail spaces, signage, textiles, fashion apparel, packaging, furniture and product design. Michael received a Bachelor of Fine Arts degree in Graphic Design from the California College of Arts & Crafts in 1968. Today he is a professor and dean of design at his alma mater (now known as California College of the Arts). In 1987 Michael was elected a member of the Alliance Graphique Internationale (AGI), an international graphic design organization based in Zurich. In addition to serving three terms on the Board of Directors of the National AIGA, he presided as president for the 2003–2005 term; he has also served on the AIGA Education Committee and was a founding member of the AIGA San Francisco Chapter. He is a professional member of the International Interior Design Association (IIDA) and in association with their Calibre Awards in 2006, the Southern California Chapter of the IIDA commended Michael with their Lifetime Achievement Award. Michael has also been honored with the Gold Medal award from AIGA and with induction into *Interior Design* Magazine's Hall of Fame.

Like a boss

by Dress Code

Some things you do with friends, other things you do with coworkers. Apparently there's a line. This is a story about crossing that line.

PROLOGUE:
We'd dreamed of having our own studio since college. Something small we could call our own, something we could plot the course of for better or worse. After we interned and worked for a number of small studios, followed by a few years in-house at a big media company, it was time to make the leap, to become a boss.

So in 2007, in our midtwenties, we rented an office, signed some official-looking paperwork and started Dress Code. In those early years, our crew was solid but small—just the two of us and some interns.

Pat had taken a few of our classes at [Insert New York Design School Name Here] and was one of those students who are a rarity in academia. He was ahead of his classmates in that he was on the forefront of creating the look that is prevalent in our industry today. Pat also didn't know how to pronounce Stefan Sagmeister's name, which gives you some idea of where his interest lay. Ask him about southern hip-hop, though, and he could screw and chop all day long. We needed him as our intern.

As Pat's tenure was nearing a close, we asked him to stay on for a bit longer. What Pat didn't know was that we were auditioning him to be our first employee. When the day came to offer Pat a spot on the team, we were nervous. Could we afford him? Would he accept? Did he even want to stay in New York? Hours after the sun set on a typical office evening, we casually mentioned that if he wanted to be our first draft pick, we would love to have him. Pat was flattered but needed some time to mull it over.

After a week or so, we got news that Pat had also been offered a job in the creative department at (Insert Hip Clothing Company Name Here). He loved us but couldn't pass up the opportunity. We were sad.

Pat had been with us for over a year, and we wanted to give him a proper send-off. We put our heads together and came up with a not-so-perfect plan.

MAIN:

How does one find a stripper you might ask? Well, this story takes place in the age of the internet, where you can find anything online with a few easy clicks. Years before, while planning our good friend's twenty-first birthday, we posted an ad on Craigslist that resulted in us interviewing a stripper toting a giant pink backpack full of dildos at the Ritz-Carlton in Lower Manhattan. But that's another story for another day.

Luckily we still had the stripper's number in our Rolodex. To up the ante we asked Stripper 1 to bring a friend, Stripper 2. In order to make this a surprise Pat would remember forever, we didn't share any of the details of what was in store on his last day at the office.

By design, part of owning our own company was not being beholden to the generally accepted start times of "corporate America." So days at Dress Code typically start around eleven. We scheduled the strippers to arrive at noon, because we thought it would be hilarious and something that cool bosses would do.

Arrive at noon the strippers did, punctual as ever, before the guest of honor, who was running wildly late, even by our lax standards.

It was hard to tell if the strippers' white Nikes and acid wash jeans were ironic or how they were living. When they mentioned it took longer than expected to get to our office from the Bronx, the answer became apparent. We directed them to the bathroom to "prepare" for the guest of honor, while we eagerly awaited his arrival.

When the ladies emerged from the bathroom, it was hard to recognize them under the facade of body glitter, pink and Lycra. They went in resembling normal girls and emerged as trashier stripper versions of themselves. The change of persona was quite impressive in a hocus-pocus kind of way.

They clip-clopped towards us like baby deer in six-inch platform acrylic heels, as unsure of their steps as they were their life choices.

We offered them seats, and there we were, along with our other interns Peg and Maz, awkwardly entertaining the two women we'd paid to entertain us. Small chat is one thing. Small chat with strippers at noon on a Wednesday is another. As the minutes ticked away on the two hours we'd purchased for these ladies' time, Pat was still nowhere to be found. Luckily Maz, who was normally a shy dude, was very adept at stripper banter.

Making things even more fun was the fact that for an hour prior to the strippers' arrival we snuck away, one-by-one, to do lines of cocaine off a CD package we'd designed in our tiny office bathroom. We were doing this on the sly from Maz, who for religious reasons didn't drink and therefore probably didn't do cocaine. Apologies in advance for stereotyping, but the covert activity was also necessary because most strippers love cocaine, and we didn't feel like going dry before 1 P.M.

To get the show moving, we frantically called Pat's cell phone and told him to jump in a cab. It was one of those hot summer days that New Yorkers dread, and he burst through the door quite sweaty. He wasn't just a little sweaty, rather he produced the kind of sweat only a hot summer sun and racing up five flights of stairs can make a man produce. Before he saw the strippers, Pat apologized profusely for being late. He thought he missed a deadline and that was the impetus for our multiple calls and texts.

That's when things got weird.

The strippers, who up until this point had been very relaxed as they drank their Red Bull and talked with Maz, switched into crazy mode and began shouting at Pat to take off his shirt. Still processing who these strangers in acrylic heels were, he turned at us, his face the perfect balance of puzzle and fright. This must have been the opening the strippers needed, because Stripper 1 leapt forward and in one motion unbuckled Pat's belt, removed it and whipped it loudly on the ground.

With the belt in hand, Stripper 1 wasn't fucking around anymore. She requested Pat's shirt. He obliged, which may not have been the strongest move, and she proceeded to whip his stomach with his belt a few more times than looked comfortable.

Stripper 2 then yelled at him to remove his pants. Stripper 1 shoved him to his knees, wrapping the belt around Pat's neck as she led him, in his boxers, around a circle on the floor. The three of us (high as hell) and Maz (hopped up on a few too many Red Bulls), watched in horror.

After what in hindsight was probably too long, one of us stepped in and put an end to the dominatrix display.

The strippers must have sensed our vibe and, to lighten the mood, suggested a game of anal ring toss.

To those of you unfamiliar with said game, it involves a stripper bending over a desk, table or other flat surface with a dildo partially up her ass. As the dildo extends beyond her ass cheeks, it creates a pole perfect for catching carnival rings.

Maz was ready to test his skill, and shortly thereafter we were all trying our hand at a few tosses. Thankfully none of us succeeded at hooking the target, because surely we didn't want to see what "winning" involved.

As the hours ticked away, the strippers did what strippers do, and things were a little less weird. They left, we laughed and kept the party going into the night, shirking our client responsibilities for the rest of

> The strippers must have sensed our vibe and, to lighten the mood, suggested a game of anal ring toss.

the day. Because, let's face it, some situations need drugs, alcohol and a little laughter thrown at them in order to be forgotten.

EPILOGUE:
And so, on that hot summer day in 2008, we learned a lesson. Just because you are the boss and can do whatever you want in your office, doesn't mean that you always should.

The names of people in this story have been changed to protect their awesomeness.

....

Dress Code is a small company that does big things for big clients: motion graphics, stop motion, and live action video.

Foie gras

by Jessica Helfand

When I was ten years old, my family moved to Paris, where we lived on a leafy, residential street in a neighborhood that, as far as I could tell, possessed absolutely no children.

Of course it was summer when we arrived, and all the little French kids were with their parents in Cannes or Biarritz or something, but all I knew was that I'd traded my street full of kids for a dull, deserted city. I went out and roller-skated anyway, hoping someone would eventually surface.

Eventually a child did emerge—and, more amazingly, she was American. Jane had a bunch of older siblings who had no interest in playing outside, but I wanted to do nothing else, so we bonded instantly. If I remember correctly, she was a little bit older, and unlike me, she already spoke French. Plus, she lived around the corner. I was delighted.

The building in which my family had settled was on a very wide street, and during the week it emptied out during the day. Evenings were a different matter, since there was a three-star restaurant that occupied the first floor of our building. There was a certain amount of well-heeled traffic in the later hours, long after I would have been in bed, and the kitchen started rumbling about noon, with young men smoking Gauloises and parking their motorbikes between the trees outside. One of them gave me a ride once.

And so it was, on a warm September afternoon—after the August silence but before school would start later in the month—that Jane and I found ourselves seriously jonesing for a snack.

"I have an idea!" squealed Jane. "Let's knock on the door of the restaurant and ask them for leftovers."

This struck me as a brilliant idea—charming and efficient, a win-win situation, as far as I could tell—made even more brilliant by the fact that Jane could ask in French. Off we went to try our luck.

In the filmstrip of my memory, the next scene goes something like this:

Jane knocks. The large front door of the restaurant opens to reveal a tall man standing in a white apron, spatula in hand, looking down at us.

"Excusez-moi, Monsieur," says Jane, "mais avez-vous du pain?"

(Excuse me, sir, but do you have any bread?)

Cut to two 10-year-olds seated at a very large round table in a small commercial kitchen. We are eating—and here, I remember the details like they happened yesterday—profiteroles and slices of a fresh baguette, with gobs of sweet strawberry jam.

Cut to my mother looking very out of place among a throng of Gauloise-smoking waiters. Next to her is the chef, who is laughing.

My mother is not laughing.

And yet, what began that day was a long and wonderful friendship between the chef (whose name was Claude Peyrot) and both my parents, but especially my mother, who Peyrot adored. After she died, I found a large envelope of his letters. They turned out to be great pals for many more years than Jane and myself.

Four years after our profiterole pit stop, my father was told he was being transferred back to the United States, and Chef Peyrot invited us to have dinner at his restaurant as his guests. By now my French was pretty much fluent, and I needed no translation for the menu.

It was all very thrilling. I had never been in the restaurant's main room, a small chic and ultramodern room with Eames furniture—and I'm pretty sure it was the first time I'd ever eaten dinner past 9 P.M. As we glanced at the menu, my father asked me what I wanted to order.

"I'm having the foie gras, to start," I announced.

My father sighed, and explained carefully that when you're the guest at a fancy restaurant, you're not supposed to order the most expensive thing on the menu.

I thought this over for a moment, looked again at the menu and then turned back to my father.

"I can't order it when you're paying, and I can't order when he's paying," I reasoned. "So when am I ever going to have it?"

I ordered the foie gras and never looked back.

....

Jessica Helfand is an award-winning graphic designer and writer. She received both her B.A. and M.F.A. from Yale University where she is senior critic in graphic design and a lecturer in Yale College. With Michael Bierut and William Drenttel, she is a founding editor of *Design Observer*, currently the largest international website for design, visual thinking and cultural criticism. A former contributing editor and columnist for *Print, Communications Arts* and *Eye* magazines, she has written for numerous national publications including *Aperture, Los Angeles Times Book Review* and *The New Republic*.

Helfand is the author of numerous books including *Screen: Essays on Graphic Design, New Media, and Visual Culture* (Princeton Architectural Press, 2001), *Reinventing the Wheel* (Princeton Architectural Press, 2002), and *Scrapbooks: An American History* (Yale University Press, 2008), which was named one of the best books of that year by *The New York Times*. Appointed by the Postmaster General to the U.S Citizens Stamp Advisory Committee in 2006, she is a Life Fellow of the American Antiquarian Society, a member of the Alliance Graphique Internationale and a recent laureate of the Art Director's Hall of Fame. With William Drenttel, Ms. Helfand was the first-ever recipient of the Henry Wolf Residency at the American Academy in Rome. In the spring of 2013, she was awarded the AIGA Medal.

Spice Girls album cover photoshoot for "Forever"

by Vince Frost

It was 2000, and I was six years into Frost*
London. One morning I had a phone call
from the marketing department at Virgin
Records UK. It was all very secret squirrel.
"We would like to talk to you about art
directing a well-known girl band's album
cover."

A few months earlier I had finished
Ronan Keating's album and singles shooting with Terry Richardson.

I was very excited about the opportunity and met with the
marketing team including "high pants" Simon Cowell. I found out
quickly that the "well-known girl band" was the Spice Girls, and
I had mixed feelings about that. I liked the scale of the fame they
had at that time, but they weren't really up my street in terms of
music interest.

I went away and started to work on a new logo and concepts
for the album cover. A couple weeks later I came back with my
ideas, which the record label liked. My ideas involved a shoot at
a modern house in the countryside and cool seventies furniture.
Immediate planning for the shoot began. It was established that we
would work with Terry Richardson and the shoot had to be within
an hour of London.

Massive amounts of meetings and planning took place. The
day arrived. Slightly nervous, I headed out of London to the site. I
arrived to see three location trucks and scores of people scurry-
ing around. Terry turned up with hundreds of boxes of disposable
cameras. Hours of makeup and wardrobe took place while the crew
patiently waited. We placed some key pieces of furniture around the
exterior of the house and checked the lighting.

Oddly I could hear people asking who I was and what I was doing there.

David Beckham turned up in his black American truck with his then very young son Brooklyn.

A panicking Virgin representative came around informing everyone that there were paparazzi hiding in the surrounding bushes.

A very surreal situation that I found slightly unnerving.

The shoot finally started and we arranged the girls in an interesting composition. Further people asked who I was and what I was doing there, and I began started to feel self-conscious and not altogether confident in what was already a tricky situation.

Terry started shooting with his disposable camera. When he finished the roll, he threw the camera in a bag each time. The light was perfect and a crew of around twenty stood behind him saying "oooh, beautiful, etc." After about half an hour of this, the marketing manager came over to me with an odd expression and said, "Vince, when is he going to use the big camera?" I said, "Those are the cameras he uses, trust him." Unconvinced, she started talking to Terry about the quality of the images and reproduction. She wasn't convinced, but the shoot continued anyway.

We broke for lunch, and I kicked a soccer ball around with David and Brooklyn for a while only to hear David ask a security guy who I was afterwards.

To cut a long story short, the shoot went on all day and at the last minute the client decided we should shoot the girls against a white wall. All those weeks of looking for furniture and locations could have been saved with me taking a picture of them against my white studio wall with a disposable camera for five pounds.

The album didn't do very well.

Some things aren't forever.

....

Vince Frost has a distinguished creative career spanning over 25 years across the globe. As a member of STD, AGI and a board member of D&AD, Vince is recognised as one of the most influential designers in the world. Vince also judges and lectures globally to diverse audiences on the value of design and the difference it can make.

My first meeting with Mr. Mick Jagger

by Stefan Sagmeister

A brand-new and extra-clean stretch limo picks me up at the studio. We are going to Newark airport. The driver hands over business class tickets for LA, and I have a stupid grin on my face all the way to the airport.

Looking out over the New Jersey industrial landscape with the Statue of Liberty at my back, I contemplate if this is one of those "happy" moments that I have about once a year.

The next morning, Jagger's assistant, Lucy, meets me in the bar, gives me a quick rundown on Mick, and we go to the suite. I'm nervous in the elevator.

Mick opens the door, turns around immediately without saying hello and I feel awkward. Lucy introduces us. He's friendly, but busy going through a Sotheby catalogue with Charlie Watts. "At nine million that's a real bargain," he says in a heavy British accent, looking at a Monet painting. "Pity I have no walls left to hang it."

I help Lucy open the water bottles. Mick grabs my portfolio and says, "So, you're the floaty one."

"The floaty one?"

"Yeah, all your covers seem to float in the plastic box."

He likes the Lou Reed package, likes the attention to detail in some of the others and I can stop being nervous. I ask him about his favorite Stones covers and he mentions without hesitation: *Exile on Main Street*, *Sticky Fingers* and *Some Girls*.

These are my favorites as well.

"We should have an easy time working together since I would have told you exactly the same covers only in a different order: *Sticky Fingers, Some Girls* and *Exile on Main Street,*" I say.

Charlie Watts (in lowered voice) asks Mick: "What's on the Sticky Fingers?" to which he replies: "Oh, you know Charlie, the one with the zipper, the one that Andy did."

The stupid happy grin is back on my face.

Jagger shows me the presentation for the stage designs, labeled "The Blasphemy Tour," with a huge baroque cross in the center of the stage. "Just look at it for style, forget about the title and the cross, we got rid of that," he says.

I mention that I'm certainly glad they did, because after having had the orthodox Hindus on my back for the use of Hindu iconography on the Aerosmith cover, I have little desire to revisit the religious world and have right-wing Christian groups making bomb threats.

Watts asks me about my accent and I tell him all about Bregenz, Austria, and that I've lived in New York for eight years, and that I'll fly back there tonight.

"Oh, you came here specially for this, so this is like a little vacation then," he says.

I tell him I feel like I've won first prize in "The Big Rolling Stones Meet the Band All Expenses Paid" radio show contest. They crack up, and I am out of there. I take the limo back to Rizzoli's, get some books on baroque, meet with the stage designers and fly out at 8:30. I feel good and am asleep before the plane leaves the ground, having learned no big lesson whatsoever.

....

Stefan Sagmeister formed the New York–based Sagmeister Inc. in 1993 and has since designed for clients as diverse as the Rolling Stones, HBO and the Guggenheim Museum. Having been nominated eight times he finally won two Grammies for the Talking Heads and Brian Eno and David Byrne package designs. He also earned practically every important international design award. In 2008, he published a comprehensive book titled *Things I have learned in my life so far* (Abrams). Solo shows on Sagmeister Inc.'s work have been mounted in Paris, Zurich, Vienna, Prague, Cologne, Berlin, New York, Miami, Los Angeles, Chicago, Toronto, Tokyo, Osaka, Seoul and Miami. He teaches in the graduate department of the School of Visual Arts in New York and lectures extensively on all continents.

In 2012, young designer Jessica Walsh became a partner and the company was renamed into Sagmeister & Walsh.

A native of Austria, Stefan received his MFA from the University of Applied Arts in Vienna and, as a Fulbright Scholar, a master's degree from Pratt Institute in New York. After his studies he worked as a creative director for Leo Burnett in Hong Kong and for M&Co. in New York.

Charlie & me

by Mick Hodgson

I met Charlie soon after he and Molly moved to Topanga in 2002. They bought a house on Bonnell, which faced a small village green and, more importantly, was one of the few flat areas in Topanga.

Because of this I used to take my young daughters down there on the weekends to learn to ride their bikes.

One Saturday a minivan pulled into the drive of the house at the end corner, which a week before had been up for sale. I watched as the car door opened and a seemingly endless stream of kids poured out, like a scene from an early silent comedy film. How many kids can you get in a minivan?

Molly walked over, and in a very warm manner that I would come to love, cheerily said hello to Lucie, the youngest of my girls who she'd met at preschool. She then went into the house and Charlie wandered over and said a quieter, more reserved hello. Mutually recognizing our English accents, we struck up more of a conversation. We walked into their house, and I asked Charlie what he did.

"I'm in the film business" he replied.

"Doing what?"

"Post production."

"Doing what?"

"I'm an editor."

"Oh, my dad was a sound editor."

"What's his name?"

"Les Hodgson."

At this reply Charlie stopped in his tracks, turned around and exclaimed: "You're Les Hodgson's son!? I worked with your dad. So you're Catherine's brother and Paul's cousin. I worked with your sister, too. That's brilliant!"

Instantly Charlie and I had a history. He was an Arsenal fan, and I was a Spurs fan, which could have been a major problem but somehow it only made our friendship that much stronger. Then we found we were both into cycling: me, mountain biking; Charlie, road. Charlie's initial reaction to that was "Mountain biking's for poofs!" but I took him on a few rides and within a year or so he would be wanting to ride on the trails, and I'd be wanting to ride on the road.

Thinking about it now, Charlie was the final piece in a puzzle I'd almost solved called living in Los Angeles. We both loved Topanga so much and for each of us when we moved to Topanga we'd arrived in heaven. We talked about this a lot when we rode, how beautiful it was, how perfect it was and how hard it would be to live anywhere better. For both of us cycling was our therapy, our antidote to the stuff we had to deal with the rest of the week.

I loved riding with Charlie and will never have as much fun as I did on my rides with him; comparing notes about the wife and kids (him moaning about Molly, me about Gill), talking about work and figuring stuff out. I remember the exact spot on a Saturday morning ride when he figured out how the whole "moving to New Zealand" plan was gong to work. (Molly had hit red tape on her New Zealand visa.) Sell the house, go to Europe, London then Italy, and if Molly couldn't get a work visa, they would stay there, he could work and more especially he could ride. "F***ing brilliant," he shouted. His handsome unshaved face beaming.

We rode nearly every weekend. If we were late starting out, he'd often bring the second of his morning espressos with him in a paper cup.

He loved all the climbs: on the road Piuma, Latigo, Deer Creek, and on his mountain bike he especially loved the park loop. And he loved to drop anyone he could, including me... especially me.

If he was on a tight schedule he'd often tell me, "Look when we get to the top I'm going to take off because Molly wants me back by eleven."

When we had dinner with him and Molly in London last summer, he was very excited about riding the Cols of the Tour de France, especially Alpe D'Huez, and he promised me he'd send a postcard.

When it arrived it was beautifully printed in neat caps, but with no house number and it said:

**AN ENGLISH GEEZER
OLDER THAN YOU MADE
IT TO THE TOP –
SO YOU'VE GOT
NO EXCUSES! I'LL
MEET YOU HERE ANYTIME
YOU CAN MAKE IT. JUST
DON'T EXPECT ME TO WAIT
FOR YOU.
–CHAS**

After Charlie died I spoke to my sister, Catherine, in London. She was particularly upset. She told me, "I loved working with Charlie, we always had such a laugh. At one point I had a real crush on him!" I told my wife, Gill, this later and she said "Well, yeah, of course, I had a crush on him, too." "Really?" I said, then I thought about it and realized, I had a crush on him, too!!

I really loved Charlie. I loved him like a brother and will miss him every day, especially every day I ride.

London born and bred Michael Hodgson (Mick to many), studied at St. Martin's School of Art and graduated from Brighton College of Art in 1974. He began his career at Harpers & Queen under the legendary Willie Landels, and served as art director until 1979, when he moved to Los Angeles. In 1988 he founded Ph.D, A Design Office, whose approach to design thinking is based on the idea of visual personalities: capturing the essence and soul of the client, and communicating those qualities throughout all applications from building signage and websites to identities, books and marketing collateral. Clients include 20th Century Fox, Chronicle Books, Frederick Fisher & Partners, The Getty Foundation, Gehry Partners LLP., Herman Miller, MasterImage 3D, Sony Corporation, and World AIDS Campaign. *Recycling & Redesigning Logos* a book Hodgson wrote and designed, was published in September 2010.

Michael is president emeritus of AIGA Los Angeles and serves on the board of Governors of OTIS College of Art & Design. In 2007, he was named an AIGA Fellow, the highest honor awarded by AIGA chapters. Most weekends he can be found on his bike riding through the canyons of the Santa Monica Mountains. Michael is married to Gill Hodgson and has three beautiful daughters: Lily, Maudie Rae, and Lucie. He always, always makes time for tea.

Origins/Orv

by Nancy Skolos

I heard a joke once: There was a zoo that had only one animal... It was a Shih Tzu.

A shit zoo pretty much describes the town I grew up in. Our small ranch house, one of sixty sitting on what was formerly a farmer's field, was a singular cage of culture—the only place where one might find a grand piano, a silkscreen print or a piece of modern furniture.

We had been located there in 1962, courtesy of my dad, Orv's, midlife crisis. After a hectic decade of working in a high-powered ad agency in a large midwestern town, he had retreated to a quieter lifestyle at a job with a company designing point-of-purchase Plexiglas signs.

His new life also had its moments of high stress. A three-pack-a-day smoker, he often spent the wee hours of the night sitting on the edge of the bed chain smoking while my mom, exhausted from teaching junior high music all day, slept in a virtual coma.

When we first moved there, a steady stream of Protestant ministers bidding for my mom's talent for directing choirs bombarded us. Orv's tactic for getting rid of them was to invite them into the not-yet-refurbished bubble gum pink living room and proceed to pick an argument about how the Immaculate Conception was impossible. The most memorable incident was the time that in the middle of one of those conversations, the cat overturned the planter/room divider, spilling vermiculite mixed with cat turds all over the carpet.

Orv and I were pretty much physical clones of each other, me being the female version of him. He, like me, was an only child and the two of us relished our mutual DNA. We enjoyed exactly the same food, had almost the same glasses prescription and compared unique foot rashes. He desperately wanted me to pursue art so I dutifully took K-12 art plus some summer classes.

His path to commercial art was made possible by World War II. He was a third-generation Norwegian who grew up in Wisconsin and didn't speak English until he went to first grade. After he joined the army, he was selected for army intelligence training at the University of Cincinnati because of his northern European appearance and his knack for speaking German. Luckily he didn't end up going abroad and after the war ended, he was invited to stay on at the university and study whatever he liked. He chose the subject of industrial design.

One of his sleepless cigarette-smoking nights was brought about by a failure in a digital clock design that employed what was at that time pretty cutting-edge technology, something the sign company cultivated to stay abreast of the competition. While my friends' chemist parents were busy keeping the Sohio refinery running, Orv was experimenting with polyurethane foam as fake wood and silk-screened vinyl as stained glass, and working on signs that used artificial fragrances to emit the smell of freshly baked cookies.

The clocks had been shipped earlier that week and a few that were delivered, caught fire at exactly 10:00.

After much mental troubleshooting, my dad had traced the design flaw to the seal between the two halves of the clock's plastic casing. If the clocks were screwed together too tightly, the light in the upper right segment of the *0* in *10:00* was in position at the edge of the box, to ignite the neoprene spacer, which he hadn't realized was flammable. He smoked through the night until morning, when the company successfully phoned all of the affected customers before 10:00 A.M.

The most outrageous assignment he ever had was to make a patch kit for John Deere's green and yellow outdoor signs, which were being shot to pieces by hunters using the logo for target practice. My dad, who wouldn't even go fishing let alone kill a deer, had the gloomy task of driving his Corvair around the county side to analyze the situation. I can just picture him on a ladder with a cigarette of mostly ashes dangling from his mouth, measuring the bullet holes. His deliverable was an elegant toolbox containing a set of hole saws in sizes to match the bullets and two rows of Plexiglas plugs in progressively sized circles, one set of green and one set of yellow. As a result, store

> The clocks had been shipped earlier that week and a few that were delivered, caught fire at exactly 10:00.

owners could easily repair the signs by sawing just the right size hole in whichever part was damaged and plugging the hole with the corresponding disk of yellow or green Plexi.

Even though I liked the trappings of commercial art—the rubber cement, the air brushes and pastels—my mother's world of music was much more attractive to me. Her choirs put on elaborate shows and went to competitions all over the state. In fourth grade, I took up the clarinet, and by high school was playing in regional bands and the youth symphony. I even went on a tour of Europe with a group of young musicians that played in Carnegie Hall, Kennedy Center and the Roman Forum. Being relatively quiet and unassuming, I lived in the expressive sounds of the clarinet, and it became my voice for both melancholy and mischief.

When it was time to go to college, I applied to three music schools as a clarinet performance major. Not realizing how many baby boomer clarinetists would be coming out of the woodwork, I chose some pretty competitive places.

My parents were still at work one day late in the spring, when I found two rejection letters in the mailbox. I ran inside the house and made a beeline for the stereo and listened to Mozart's Clarinet Concerto while sobbing face down into the living room carpet. My two surrogate siblings, Hilde the dachshund, and Joe the cat, were stunned by this unusual display of emotion and sat side by side next to my head, lending sympathy. When the piece was over, I collected myself, found my application materials and dialed the conservatory at the University of Cincinnati, the one school that I hadn't been rejected from yet. A nice woman answered, "Hello?"

"Would you send my application for the music school over to the design school?" I asked.

"What kind of design do you want?"

"What kind do you have?"

"Fashion?"

"No."

"Interior?"

"No."

"Industrial?"

"Yes."

That would work. That is what Orv had done.

Nancy Skolos works with her husband Thomas Wedell to diminish the boundaries between graphic design and photography—creating collaged three-dimensional images influenced by modern painting, technology and architecture. With a home/studio halfway between Boston and Providence they balance their commitments to professional practice and teaching at the Rhode Island School of Design where Skolos is a professor and Wedell is a senior visiting critic.

Their clients have included Boston Acoustics, Callaway Editions, Cambridge Arts Council, Digital Equipment Corporation, EMI Music Publishing, Harvard Medical School, Hasbro Inc, U.S. Department of Health and Human Services, Industrial Designers Society of America, Lyceum Fellowship, Maine Lakes Conservancy, Reinhold Brown Gallery, Rhode Island School of Design, Steelcase Design Partnership and the U.S. Postal Service.

The studio's work has received numerous awards the including a Silver Prize 1985 in Toyama, a Bronze Prize in Lahti 1988 Silver Prize in 2011, and a Gold Medal in Warsaw in 2010; and has been widely published and exhibited. Skolos/Wedell's posters are included in the graphic design collections of the Museum of Modern Art, The Israel Museum, Jerusalem and the Museum für Gestaltung, Zurich, Switzerland. Skolos is an elected member of the Alliance Graphique Internationale and a Boston AIGA Fellow.

Mr. McCormick and the case of the very large television set

by Chris Coyier

I roll up to Scott's house at about seven in the morning. I think my text woke him up. He has me wait outside while he gets ready to go.

His is the kind of house on the kind of street where the creaky gate pushes away some beers cans in order to open. Scott looks like he has seen better mornings, but his gear is absolutely ready to go.

About five hours later there is a television the size of a European car just about to shatter onto the sidewalk right as his camera shutter clicks.

Scott is a photographer buddy of mine in Denver, Colorado. I needed some photos taken of me for a magazine interview. I can't

Photo: Scott McCormick

imagine a more uncomfortable thing to do. I was driving through Denver on a road trip when it clicked that Scott could shoot the photos. That would be a lot easier and more comfortable than hiring some Craigslist photographer.

I'm not sure what people think when they first meet Scott. They might assume he's a hard-living kind of guy. He was in touring bands for a long time. He's gone through some tough family stuff. He's still young but has some lines under the eyes and a huge natural beard. He wears plaid shirts and cutoff shorts. Thick-framed glasses. He's as nice as the day is long.

We have no solid plan for this photo shoot. The first place we decide to head is Red Rocks. Google some pictures of it if you've never been there. It's a crazy beautiful music venue in the middle of some huge rock formations. When there isn't a concert you can walk around and check it out for free. We think some photos there might be cool. We take about three photos before the moms pushing strollers up and down the rows, runners bounding up the steps and tourists staring at each other has us bolting for the exit.

Scott isn't a "let's find a pretty brick wall" kind of photographer (by a long shot). He likes to get weird. Lots of action, props and compositing.

Scott has an idea to go to Goodwill, a resale shop that takes in donated clothes and housewares and sells them at low prices. The plan is simple. We're going to buy a truckload of stuff, find a building, get the stuff on the roof, throw it off and take pictures of it. I think it's brilliant in the raw, sort of dumb, juvenile-ness of it. It's sure to make for some fun photos. We'll also get some photos of me walking past the building. Then Scott will composite the photos to make it seem like the stuff is falling on me. Like every time I walk past this damn building I end up in the middle of some domestic dispute a few stories up.

I have to slam my shoulder into the truck door leaving Goodwill to get it to close. We bought so much crap we almost have to make two trips. Of course it doesn't help that the bed of the truck is almost entirely taken up by this huge tube television from the eighties. I wish I had a photo of my dog Digby squished in the backseat. She isn't especially pleased.

The first hiccup in this plan is that we don't actually know of a building that we can use to throw all of this crap off of.

So we just start driving around different neighborhoods in Denver. Scott is looking at buildings and judging them by how they would look in the shot, while I'm secretly a little more concerned about whether the owner of the building is going to let us essentially sprinkle broken glass all over their parking lot. Just rolling with it is key to hanging out with Scott.

We find the perfect building in a residential neighborhood. Only two stories, but tall enough that you won't be able to see the top or sides in the photos that Scott envisions. He marches up and knocks on the door. Turns out, it's this old hippy-looking dude's house and the Scott even knows him. Greg was his name. He designed an album cover for a band Scott was in years ago. Small world. He didn't hesitate to say yes.

The second hiccup is that there was no way to get onto the roof. Scott talks Greg into driving over to his brother's place to get us a ladder, and in the meantime, we pick up and move his garden shed up against the side of the building. When he gets back, he just kinda shrugs, and we put the ladder on top of the garden shed and that gets us on the roof. Hot tar, of course.

It gets a little tricky now. We are able to carry bags of clothes and books and random junk up the ladder pretty easily, but this baby whale of a television is another story. One guy couldn't lift it on flat ground. The first idea is to take it apart a bit, but that is scrapped because we want the TV to look like it's in good shape on the way down. Besides, the easy parts to take off don't weigh much anyway. The second idea is to tie it up with ropes and yank it up from the top. Scott and I are able to yank it up about half way before it is just too hard. I totally give up at this point. It seems really hopeless to me. But Scott is already on the phone with other guys to come help. Just minutes later we have a third guy on the roof (Punk

Rock Tom, of course), helping us yank this thing up. We get it to the top edge but fail to realize how hard it's going to be to angle it over the edge. Scott ends up kind of dangling off the side of the building to try and reach underneath it and heft it up. Wildly dangerous, but somehow it works and only cost him only a pinky fingernail.

Should we have thought about it longer, I think the third idea would have been sliding it up the ladder at an angle that would have made that last part a lot easier.

The actual photo-taking process goes like this: I walk by the building front doing something typical like talking on the phone, walking my dog or just sitting on the curb on my laptop. Scott has his camera taped to another ladder in front of the house, so it remains absolutely still between shots. (Somehow the most cringe-worthy part of this story is imagining the duct tape residue that's probably still on that multithousand-dollar camera.) Then as soon as the photo of me is snapped, I sprint around the house, up the ladder and start chucking stuff off while Scott takes more photos. If they don't look quite right, he chucks the stuff back up to me and I throw it off again.

Timing is everything. Scott's camera is awesome but it's not the kind that takes a ton of shots super quickly. He has to click it at just the right second. Not only does he need to have perfect timing, but the sun is setting. That affects the light in the shots. At noon, the light is relatively stable, but as the sun sets, the lighting changes more quickly, so we only have a few minutes to make each shot. Otherwise, the pictures would be impossible to composite together.

The television is the last shot. By this time, the neighbors have gathered in the streets to watch the shenanigans. They cheer when the television is hefted onto the ledge. We figure out just where it is likely to fall, and then I sit in that spot on the curb for the first photo. Once we get that, I run around the house, up onto the roof, and boot the TV off the roof like Gerard Butler booted that Persian emissary into the death well in *300*.

Click.click.click.click.

I don't know if you've ever thrown a tube television off a roof, but wow, if you land it just right it sounds like a bomb going off. People

will hit the deck, if they aren't ready for it. The "tube" part is a "cath-ode ray tube." I think Wikipedia says it best:

"If the glass is damaged, atmospheric pressure can collapse the vacuum tube into dangerous fragments which accelerate inward and then spray at high speed in all directions."

Indeed.

We go and rent a shop vac and spend the next several hours vacuuming glass shards out of Greg's parking area. But, hey, we got the shot!

Chris Coyier is a web designer and developer. He writes about all thing web at CSS-Tricks and talks about all things web at conferences around the world and on his podcast *ShopTalk*. He co-founded the web coding playground CodePen.

Applause sounds same in every language

by Hideki Nakajima

It was 1996. As an art director in Tokyo, I was challenged to enter NYADC, one of the world's toughest design competitions. I was really curious to see how my designs would be judged.

One day an invitation to attend the prize giving arrived but I didn't know if I would be awarded a prize or not. I might have to fly back empty-handed.

But thinking, *Hey, what the hell?*, I took a risk and got a flight to New York.

Essex House, the venue for NYADC, was so luxurious and full of so many famous faces, but I had no idea who most of them were. It was like a scene from some movie. I also don't speak English (my translator's writing this, by the way), so I had no idea what was going on or how to deal with any of it. By then, I had the impression that I wouldn't receive a prize especially among so many legendary people. *Forget about it; just enjoy yourself and have a good time,* I decided, determined to take pleasure in the atmosphere if nothing else.

There were so many other good works presented onscreen. Sooner or later, it was the category I had entered and all of a sudden I realized that it was my work on the screen! I could hear my name being called so I jumped up from my seat and ran on stage.

The presenter kindly whispered that I should go back to my seat and simply bow; I'd won the silver medal.

Yes, silver medal! I was so happy but at the same time so mortified by my mistake that my face was literally on fire with embarrassment.

Right after this happened, I was awarded another silver medal. I had already learned my lesson so this time I simply stood up and bowed politely with my face still blushing.

Then at the very end of the ceremony, the last and best award was announced, the gold medal. And it was me! Prompted, I left my seat and stepped onto the stage where the presenter whispered to me again, "Welcome back."

With much applause and many cheers, I was as happy as a clown could be with the crown in his hand. I could finally communicate with all these wonderful people not by spoken word but through my work. It gave me so much confidence back then. I am, however, still not able to speak English.

To be continued...

Hideki Nakajima established Nakajima Design in 1995. Exhibitions include the 2004 Nakajima Design Exhibition at the Guangzhou Musuem for Art, the 2006 CLEAR in the FOG Hideki Nakajima Exhibition at Ginza graphic gallery, the 2009 Collection Hideki Nakajima Exhibition at The OCT Art & Design Gallery, and Hideki Nakajima 1992-2012 at Daiwa Press Viewing Room.

Past awards include the Art Directors Club Awards 5 Gold and 7 Silver Prizes, the Tokyo Art Directors Club awards (1999) the Tokyo Art Directors Club Hiromu Hara Awards (2007, 2012), the Chicago Athenaeum Good Design Award, the Kodansha Publishing Cultural Award, the 3rd International Poster Biennial Ningbo (2004) and Tokyo Type Directords Club Awards Grand Prix (2006) in addition to many other awards across the world.

Nakajima's art works are held in many museums worldwide as permanent collections. His work is published in the *Revival* anthology (1999), *CLEAR in the FOG*" (2006), *TYPO-GRAPHICS Hideki Nakajima* (2008), *Hideki Nakajima 1992-2012* (2012), and many others. Member of AGI (Alliance Graphique Internationale Swissland), The Art Directors Club (New York), Tokyo Art Directors Club and Tokyo Type Directords Club.

The Devil made him do it

by Carin Goldberg

In the fall of 1985, when Ed Koch was Mayor of New York and the AIDS crisis was beginning to take its toll on the city's gay community, my husband, James Biber, and my best friend from Cooper Union, Gene Greif, and I moved into the top floor of 270 Lafayette Street, a mostly unoccupied building located on the cusp of Soho and Nolita. We were among the first professional tenants to move into one of the many raw spaces in a neighborhood that would gentrify at the speed of sound and become a neighborhood of style and commerce and prohibitive rents.

At the time, Gene, always looking for a distraction from work, took it upon himself to persuade the landlord to let him use one of the empty spaces in the building to make a large-scale project for the upcoming Greenwich Village Halloween Parade. A spectacle stretching for more than a mile, this yearly event began in 1974, attracted thousands of spectators and costumed participants, floats, and a worldwide television audience, and was not for pussies. If you were going to participate you had to embrace it with fearless creativity and audacity. Gene was the man for the job, but for him there would be no rubber masks of Koch or Reagan, and no drag in this gayest

MONSTERS PROWL CITY

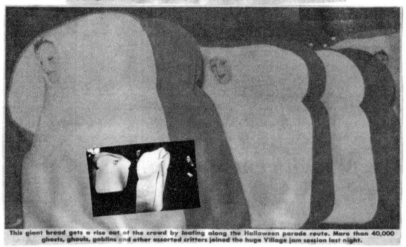

This giant bread gets a rise out of the crowd by loafing along the Halloween parade route. More than 40,000 ghosts, ghouls, goblins and other assorted critters joined the huge Village jam session last night.

NEW YORK POST, TUESDAY, NOVEMBER 1, 1983

of Halloween rituals. His idea was to construct ten, seven-foot-tall slices of Wonder Bread made from white foam rubber and brown spray paint for the crusts. Jim, Gene, and I along with seven of our friends would be completely cloaked short of our faces peering out of a hole cut in the front of our costumes.

Our mutual best friend, Neil, another talent with hands of gold and a brilliant wit, decided he would not participate in this group endeavor. He would go his own way this time around, choosing to masquerade as "The Devil with the Blue Dress." Neil can sew, sculpt, draw and paint masterfully so there was no doubt that his creation would be beautifully made and hysterically funny.

With the craftsmanship of a couture seamstress, he made a stunning blue satin and organza gown. He painted his skin bright red and wore black, hardware-heavy, calf-high combat boots. A three-foot-long serpentine tail punctuated the costume with humor and charm. Neil arrived with a boom box strapped to his shoulder and a looped tape of the song "Devil with the Blue Dress On" (the 1966 hit, recorded by Mitch Ryder and The Detroit Wheels) poised to blast through the crowd. Neil was confident that his clever costume would blow this goofy loaf of bread marching ahead of him right off Bleecker Street.

But what Neil didn't anticipate was that his red makeup would read as black under the yellow sodium streetlights, and that the deafening din of the crowd chanting "BREAD! BREAD! BREAD!" for the *entire* duration of the parade would completely obliterate the song from Neil's boom box. No one knew what Neil was; most just thought he was a six-foot three-inch man in drag with skin inexplicably painted black.

Neil was devastated, mortified. Making things worse, the next day a banner photo of all of us, the entire loaf, appeared in *The New York Post*.

While the Devil may have been a more timely comment on the politics of 1985, at a time when Act Up proclaimed that Sex=Death, maybe a giant loaf of soft, comforting white bread was just the thing this crowd hungered for.

Coda: The following Halloween we were a giant Carvel ice cream cake.

Neil was one of six slices.

....

Carin Goldberg was born in New York City and studied at the Cooper Union School of Art.

She began her career as a staff designer at CBS Television, CBS Records and Atlantic Records before establishing her own firm, Carin Goldberg Design, in 1982.

Over the following two decades Carin designed hundreds of book jackets for every major American publishing house. In recent years her image making has expanded to publication design, brand consulting, poster design and illustration.

In 2009 she was awarded the prestigious AIGA Gold Medal. In 2008 Carin completed a two-year term as president of the New York Chapter of the American Institute of Graphic Arts. She also served on the chapter's board from 2002 to 2004. In 2009, she was awarded the Cooper Union President's Citation for exceptional contributions to the field of graphic design. She has been a member of the Alliance Graphique Internationale (AGI) since 1999 and served on its board of directors from 2006-2009. From November 2010–January 2011, a retrospective of her work and career was exhibited at Musée Géo-Charles, Échirolles, France.

Carin teaches typography, editorial design, senior thesis and design history at the School of Visual Arts in New York and is one of the first recipients of the Art Directors Club Grandmasters Award for Excellence in Education (2008).

She and her husband, architect James Biber, live and work in Manhattan.

Brad

by DJ Stout

The bar was noisy, and even though Brad was screaming at the top of his lungs at the pudgy investment banker–type, I couldn't make out a single word.

It was clear that he was keyed up, though, and when both men began to lean across the pool table toward one another, their faces inches apart and their eyes locked in a deadly mano-a-mano stare-down, I knew we were in trouble. Truth be told, I was under the influence of several Pabst Blue Ribbons, so that and the heat and deafening roar of the Friday night crowd made my head spin. It happened in seconds, but in my fuzzy memory it seemed like a slow-motion dream sequence. I remember a fist hurtling toward Brad's face and my instinctive lunge across the pool table to intercept it. Then everything came unglued. People started screaming, chairs and tables turned over, pool sticks snapped, and somehow I ended up in a dog pile on the ground, my face smashed down into the grimy beer-soaked floor. The next thing I knew, I was being carried aloft through the bar by two beefy bouncers, and when they reached the front door, they threw my ass out onto the icy pavement. My illustrator friend Anita Kunz followed, and while I was brushing myself off and trying to regain my composure from that demeaning event, she started shrieking. "Oh my God, DJ! What happened? Oh my God! Where's Brad? He's still in there!" Then Brad, escorted by the bouncers, emerged with a big grin on his face and blood oozing down his chin onto his dapper winter scarf.

My troublemaking friend was Brad Holland, one of the greatest illustrators of our time, and he's been known to tell that story on more than one occasion, but with a slightly different slant—let's just say with more of a northerner's perspective. According to Brad's narrative, he was having a beer at Hogs and Heifers, a sort of southern

"

I remember a fist hurtling toward Brad's face and my instinctive lunge across the pool table to intercept it. Then everything came unglued.

"

redneck bar located in the now fashionable Meat District of New York City, and since he was with a Texas art director—and you know how much Texans love bar brawls—I was the one who threw the first punch. That's not how I remember it, but it does make for an entertaining Tall Texas Tale.

I first encountered Brad Holland's art in *Playboy*, illicitly of course, when I was twelve years old but later, during my first semester in college, I happened on a drawing he did for the *New York Times*. I remember that moment clearly because the quarter-page op-ed piece reached out and grabbed me by the throat. The small pen-and-ink composition, a gritty depiction of a crazy-eyed junkie cinching a belt around his bicep with his teeth and feeding spoonfuls of drugs to four gaping mouths protruding from his arm, made me crazy with envy. It was a raw, gut-wrenching drawing, rendered so sure-handedly in thick layers of crosshatching, that it became my holy grail.

Brad's style is so confident, so unique, and so utterly original that it's as if it burst forth from the man fully developed. There doesn't seem to have been a trial-and-error period, no process of gestation. Brad claims he was influenced by Goya, but I don't see it. I know he works hard at his craft. I've observed him in his studio, working and reworking an image, perfecting a troublesome minor element or painting over an entire composition that looked perfectly fine to me. By the time I landed my first graphic design job in Dallas, Brad Holland had reached a divine status. In my mind he was a supreme being, a deity. He was the god of illustration. He even looked the part, with his scruffy holy-man beard, his long stringy hair perpetually falling over his dark beady eyes, and his strong, noble nose that could easily belong to an Afghan warlord. His normal expression, dead serious with brief interludes of a wicked smile, and his relentless unblinking gaze is unsettling at first encounter. Actually, I always thought he looked like the devil, a handsome devil but satanic just the same. I was truly in awe of the man, but he scared the shit out of me.

Toward the end of my stint as art director of Robert A. Wilson Associates in Dallas, I got the assignment to design an important annual report for Robert Jarvik, M.D., the flashy inventor of the first successful artificial heart, and his new company, Symbion. In 1982 the Jarvik 7 device had been successfully transplanted into a retired dentist named Barney Clark, to much fanfare, and the achievement transformed Dr.

Jarvik into an instant medical celebrity. The Jarvik heart, powered by a clunky shopping cart–sized apparatus, severely restricted the patient's mobility and was plagued with other problems, but it was a remarkable first step and a rocket shot into a brave new world. Jarvik and William DeVries, M.D., who performed the implant surgery, held daily press conferences to brief the ravenous media who was captivated by the story. Barney Clark died after 112 days, but in 1985 the second Jarvik 7 was implanted in a patient named Bill Schroeder, who suffered a debilitating stroke two weeks later but lived with the artificial heart for 620 days. A year later Dr. Jarvik became the chairman and CEO of Symbion, Inc., a public company that was set up to manufacture the Jarvik 7 heart, and that's when I entered the picture.

The idea that a man, a mere mortal, had developed a machine that could replace the human heart, the remarkable and mysterious nucleus of life, was seen as nothing less than a miracle. In 1982 the ethics and morality of Dr. Jarvik's game-changing artificial heart were being debated all over the world, so I came up with the concept of inviting a half-dozen experts to write opinion pieces for the Symbion annual report. We invited medical specialists, newspaper columnists, religious leaders and magazine journalists, and then I commissioned six of the top illustrators in the country to create full-page black and white thought pieces to accompany them. Like the articles featured in the op-ed pages of the *New York Times*, we encouraged the guest authors to comment on the controversial medical phenomenon from their well-informed points of view, without a corporate agenda, and the illustrators were free to do the same. My idea was for Symbion to embrace the worldwide debate, to jump into the fray with both feet, and to become a part of the conversation instead of ignoring it. The notion was to wallow in the controversy and to provide an open forum for honest opinions, even if one of the participants took a negative view of Symbion's products or questioned the company's ethics. It was a totally different, and refreshingly editorial, approach to a corporate annual report.

Brad Holland, who had been a frequent contributor to the *New York Times* op-ed pages, and who famously waged a personal war against Richard Nixon during the Watergate hearings with his scathing visual commentary, featured daily in that influential section of the paper, was the first potential contributor I considered for the Symbion annual report. (Ironically, years later Brad became an admirer and a scholar, actually a super fan, of Richard Nixon.) The Jarvik heart was rich subject matter, and the Symbion annual report, as I had conceived it, was the perfect forum for the master illustrator. But I was terrified to make the call. Brad looked mean and unapproachable to me—he was the devil incarnate—and his steadfast insistence on his way or the highway, a personality trait that preceded the legendary New York artist, was intimidating for a greenhorn art director who had just begun working for a small corporate communications firm down in Texas.

When I finally called Brad, it could not have been a more pleasant experience. He was friendly and soft-spoken and seemed genuinely enthusiastic about the project. We talked at length about the game-changing artificial heart and its implications on society and the world of medicine, but the aspect of the assignment he liked the most was the total freedom I gave him. It was my first experience commissioning a great illustrator, and the truth is, I didn't know any better. He was the experienced one, a seasoned pro, so I couldn't imagine telling him how to do his job. It was the first of many fruitful and satisfying experiences I've had over the years working with some of the best illustrators in the world. My philosophy has never wavered from that day on. Hire a talented, proven illustrator, and get the hell out of the way.

Brad sent me a wonderful full-page pen-and-ink drawing of a hawk in the shape of a heart, and I got great contributions from the other illustrators I commissioned for the project, including Geoffrey Moss, who had waged his own personal war against Richard Nixon in the pages of the *Washington Post*. When I sent the blue-line of the annual report to Symbion, the only comment I got back was a silly request to remove Brad Holland's signature because it was fairly prominent and they thought it was inconsistent with the other illustrations. I explained how Brad Holland's signature actually added value to their annual report, but they insisted. Now, I was young and naive and severely technically challenged, and my only real publication design experience had been with college newspapers, so I took an X-acto knife, sliced Brad's signature out of his original pen-and-ink drawing, and sent it back to the printer.

On the night of the press run for the Symbion annual report, I was filled with anticipation. I couldn't believe it was just hours from getting printed. It was an original timely piece of communication for an annual report, and it had miraculously survived the gauntlet of corporate approvals that, in my opinion, exist only to destroy creativity.

I was about to go to bed to get some rest before the early morning press check—and then the phone rang. It was Symbion calling, and they wanted to stop the presses.

My real heart skipped a beat. I couldn't believe what I was hearing. Dr. Jarvik had looked at the final blue-line, and now he wanted the opinion pieces replaced with new corporate copy, hastily thrown together by the in-house marketing team, and the full-page illustrations switched out with photographs of the senior management team, including a predictable portrait of himself, sitting smugly in a constipated crossed-arm pose.

There was no official explanation for the baffling change of course, but years later, I discovered that a hostile takeover of Symbion had occurred right around that time. So the last-minute pulling of the plug had something to do with politics, no doubt. Dr. Jarvik was about to lose his fledgling company, and he was doing whatever he could to hold on. Bob Wilson was furious. He had personally invited many of the guest authors to contribute to the project, and now he had to call each of them to deliver the embarrassing news. But the first call he made was to Symbion, Inc., which he fired over the phone with a flare that filled my heart with self-righteous glee. I had to call all the illustrators too, of course, but being professionals with much more experience than I, they all took it in stride.

After several weeks, the memory of the Symbion annual report debacle joined the ranks of the many rejected and forgotten projects that inhabit the island of lost designs. But then one day I got a call from Brad Holland, the devil himself, and he was mad as hell. He had just received my package in the mail, and when he pulled out the pen-and-ink drawing he had created for the Symbion annual report, he saw that some asshole had taken a knife and gouged out his signature from the bottom right-hand corner of his original piece of art. Brad was incredulous. He just couldn't believe it. How could anybody be that stupid and careless? It was bad enough that the piece was never going to be published, but now his one-of-a-kind drawing was ruined. Who was responsible for such a hackneyed, irresponsible, act of ignorance? He demanded. And so I did what any self-respecting art director would do. I blamed it on the printer.

DJ Stout is one of nineteen principals of the acclaimed international design consultancy Pentagram. Stout joined Pentagram as a partner in 2000. Pentagram, which was founded in London in 1972 by five designers—an architect, a product designer and three graphic designers—currently has five offices around the world. In a special 1998 issue, *American Photo* magazine selected DJ as one of the 100 most important people in photography. In 2004, *I.D. (International Design)* magazine selected Stout for The I.D. Fifty, it's annual listing of design innovators. In 2010 The Society of Illustrators honored DJ Stout with the national Richard Gangel Art Director Award. Also in 2010, DJ Stout was recognized as an AIGA (American Institute of Graphic Arts) Fellow award recipient for his exceptional contributions to the field of graphic design.

DJ and his team specialize in the creation of brand identity design and strategy, publication design, packaging and interactive solutions. Recent projects include World Wildlife Fund, Microsoft Windows Vista, Ruby Tuesday Restaurants, Popeyes Louisiana Kitchen, Walgreens, L.L. Bean, Southwest Airlines, Perot Museum of Nature and Science, SkinCeuticals, Drexel University, Loyola Marymount University and The University of Southern California.

A dog's tale

by Richard van der Laken

Years ago, in the nineties, when I was still a young man ;-) I did an internship at the renowned studio of Dutch graphic designer Anthon Beeke.

In the center of Amsterdam, he ran a creative studio and worked for highbrow clients like the Stedelijk Museum Amsterdam, Li Edelkoort's Trend Union in Paris and Holland's biggest theatre group Toneelgroep Amsterdam.

At that time I had a little dog, a Jack Russell terrier called Bobo. Together with my dog, I visited the studio and, in my naivety, applied for this internship. Luckily everybody fell in love with Bobo. So I was hired!

Bobo was so charming that everybody in the studio always forgave his untamable urge to bark, his unstoppable lust for food from trash cans and fights with other much, much bigger dogs. Nevertheless, during my internship at this God of Graphic Design, my dog gave me many almost heart attacks.

Within the walls of the studio, Bobo had a refined sense of sticking his wet nose into things he should not stick it in.

One time, Anthon was working on one of his famous posters for theater group Toneelgroep Amsterdam. (During my internship it really was a treat to see magic happen. Anthon always photographed them himself. And sometimes he asked me to assist him.) This time it was a poster for *Othello*. He photographed a close-up of an eye, with tears. A very simple but striking image. And it was in the good old off-line, analog, manual time with Kodak and Fuji small film.

After we wrapped up the shoot, Anthon asked me to bring the film to the lab for developing. So I did of, course. A day later I picked it up from the lab and put the film roll on Anthon's desk. At a certain moment Anthon asked me where I left the film.

. . . .

And precisely at that moment I saw Bobo in the corner of the studio chewing on something that looked like ... the film roll.

. . . .

And, of course, it was the film roll.

I thought I would die there on the spot.

I grabbed the leftovers and gave them to Anthon, expecting that this was my last minute at his studio.

Anthon looked at the leftovers, looked at Bobo, looked at me and then started to laugh. He took a pair of scissors and cut out the last three images that were not damaged by Bobo's jaws. The result: an award-winning poster.

The Dutch graphic design studio Designpolitie (Richard van der Laken and Pepijn Zurburg) is celebrated for its fresh, deceptively simple and direct approach to graphic design, which often implements bright color and sans-serif typeface in a lively and fun style.

Among other projects, Designpolitie (Designpolice) is behind the review column Gorilla in the Dutch newspaper *De Volkskrant* and weekly magazine *De Groene Amsterdammer*, in which the team reacts to current affairs with word-and-image graphics.

Their monograph *The ABC of De Designpolitie* is an index of Designpolitie's reflections on design, catalogued in humorously alphabetical order (with failed projects filed under "Damn," or an account of their simplified methods under "Rocket Science"). More of a workbook, a process book or an inspirational resource than a portfolio, The ABC collates Designpolitie projects (implemented and otherwise), schemes, photographs, musings and articles in a style that is both serious and replete with irony and self-mockery—a natural extension of the firm's own ethos.

Richard and Pepijn are also the initiators, curators and designers of a new major international designconference about the impact of design, called What Design Can Do.

As Designpolitie Richard and Pepijn exhibited in the Stedelijk Museum Amsterdam, the Graphic Design Museum Breda, the Design Museum London, the New York MoMA, the San Francisco MoMA, Institut Neerlandais Paris, Brno Tsjechia and the Milan Triennale.

They published their work in numerous Dutch, European, American, Chinese and Japanese magazines and books. In November 2008 their monograph 'The ABC of De Designpolitie' came out.

Richard and Pepijn frequently lecture and give workshops in The Netherlands, Belgium, Spain, Denmark, Italy, Serbia, Norway, Sweden, the U.K, Poland, South Africa, Brazil, and India.

Richard and Pepijn were honored with different grants from the The Netherlands Foundation for Visual Arts, Design and Architecture (known in the Netherlands as Fonds BKVB) and won numerous Design Awards and merits. These include the Dutch Art Directors Club (ADCN), Dutch Best Book Design, Dutch Housestyle Awards, Dutch Design Awards, Red Dot Awards, British D&AD, New York ADC and the European Design Awards.

They were jurymembers at the Dutch Design Awards, the Eurobest Designcontest, the British D&AD and the Norwegian Visuellt.

Über

by Randy Hunt

We're revamping the design space at the office. I've got a couple of boxes, mostly books, and I need to transport them from home.

I'm a New Yorker without a car, common scenario, and I need to move something that one person can't easily carry on the subway or bus. Time to get a car service.

Of late, I've been using an app on my phone that makes it super-duper easy to get a car service. Simply set your pick up location and tap to request a car. This is going to sound like an infomercial for the service, Über, but it's important that I explain the details of how this works just a little bit more.

The car service world is very fractured and doesn't really work to the passenger's favor. Typically a passenger would call a phone number they have on file for a car service, whose drivers are generally dispatched from a particular neighborhood. The dispatcher on the phone will give you a time estimate, usually "five minutes! five minutes!" which can mean anything from three minutes to about fifteen minutes, depending on the service you called, traffic, the driver's familiarity with your area, etc. The passenger typically doesn't know who the driver will be, what the car will look like, how far away they actually are, when they'll arrive or if the driver is safe and reliable. It's a big black cloud of mystery (and sometimes the smell of cigarette smoke) all the way through the transaction—usually cash only—when the driver tells you how much your ride will cost.

An experienced car-service user knows to confirm the price with the driver before getting in, otherwise, you have no idea how much it'll cost. A service like Über fundamentally disrupts this model in almost every way.

First, calling a car: You choose where you want to be picked up by placing a pin on a map, choosing a location from Foursquare's database or entering an address. If you know your destination, you can enter that as well and get a fare estimate before you ever request a car.

Speaking of being informed, once you've requested a car on Über, you can see the current location of the car as it's making its way to you—a happy little black rectangle of information scooting its way across the map. Should you choose to not stare at a map on your phone for ten minutes, the driver triggers a text message as the car is arriving, letting you know your ride will be there momentarily. This is great if you're waiting inside, safe from the weather or if you are soaking in one last goodbye.

You're greeted by a very, very clean car, much cleaner than the what you'd expect from a car service in New York City. Sometimes they even have amenities like bottles of water or a good magazine to peruse.

When you're done with your unusually plush ride, you have to settle up, and this is equally as impressive. Über lets you pay by credit card, and you don't have to have your credit card on you. You save it in the app, can choose the card on file you want and when your ride is done you simply get out of the car. No need to pull your card out, no fumbling for cash.

A receipt is emailed to you, and you have the opportunity to rate and leave feedback on your driver. Awesome.

I had heard rumors that car drivers didn't like it, and I couldn't understand why. I suppose disruptive change is always threatening to the establishment. I always got in an Über car thinking that drivers go along with the technology but don't necessarily love it. *They're probably ambivalent*, I thought.

Now, back to me, my boxes, and my need to move them to the office... I got a text message, hauled the boxes to the curb and the car arrived right on time. As I was used to at this point, the driver asked me about Über, how long I've been using it, how I love it. Unlike other drivers recently, he spoke up about his thoughts. Excited, elated even, he proceeded to tell me that he loves it too. "It's so easy. It's so easy," he said with childlike enthusiasm and wonder.

We continued to chitchat for a bit. Eventually, we just let the conversation rest. You know the feeling. I'm riding in a car with a total stranger. At some point, you don't have much more to talk about.

We rode for another five minutes or so, zipping along the highway in silence. Then, all of a sudden, he broke the silence: "There are four things that have changed mankind!"

I was taken aback, and he was about to drop some unsolicited personal philosophy on me. "Okay ..." and before I can possibly show interest—and believe me, I was interested—he proceeded to tell me.

"One, the Bible."

Already I was wondering, *Where is this conversation going?*

"Two, the American Constitution." This was interesting because I believed his accent to be German. At this point, I was thinking that he's all about historical texts or something. I didn't have time to make sense of where he was.

"Three, Google!"

The driver had his chronology going at this point, so I was thinking, *What could possibly be number four?*

"Four…Über!"

It's easy to look at the things that exist and think they're established, unwavering and simply the way things are. But they can change right underneath you. We can change them, in ways that bring a smile to people's faces. Design can do that. (Props to the designers of Über.)

Randy Hunt is creative director at Etsy, where he leads a team of designers creating the end-to-end experience, both online and off. Hunt feels strongly that designers must be able to build what they design, a perspective that fits naturally with Etsy's culture of making and the love of craftsmanship. Hunt cofounded Supermarket, a curated design marketplace. Previously, he founded Citizen Scholar Inc. and worked at Milton Glaser Inc. and Number 17. He writes and lectures about design and has been a visiting designer and critic at many colleges and universities.

Save me the aisle seat

by Rick Valicenti

It was Friday, April 19, 2013. After a long week in the Thirst Studio and I needed a bit of good, clean performance art.

I made a spontaneous decision to head over to the MCA Stage, where for sixty minutes six nude women would perform *Untitled Feminist Show*, the intensely resonant work by the Shakespearean scholar, Korean-American playwright-director Young Jean Lee.

"One ticket, please." My seat was on the right aisle in row I, a really good midsection seat in an almost full auditorium. The stage was as bare as the subjects who performed with virtually no recognizable dialogue, yet the actors seemed to have plenty to say through body language pulsating to synchronized music.

About two-thirds of the way through the piece, the short, long-haired brunette woman was all alone and the ambient, amplified din morphed into a heavy metal slashing roar. With each increase in volume, this actress thrashed about, throwing herself from one side of the stage to the other—and finally right off the edge. Damn, if the front row didn't have the spectacle of this whirling dervish from WWF within arms reach. Back and forth. Back and forth until, she took to the stairs on the right side, thrashing and crashing against the wall as if she was channeling Linda Blair. *WTF!*

With a sudden force, she grabbed me with both hands at the back of my head and slammed me face-first into her sweaty cleavage.

Pulling. Pushing. Then she let go of my head and shoved my shoulders back into the back of the wooden auditorium chair. In a split second, I was yanked forward again into her body as she pummeled my back. And, as if there was not enough insult heaped on to me, she tossed my head from side to side in some sort of chiropractic madness before I was dismissed for limp. Then she head banged herself back onto the stage.

OMG! I was grateful it was pretty dark in the theater.

The next morning, I Googled her, checked out her blog on motion art and sent her an email. Fortunately her name was in the evening's program, which I still had in my possession. As an attachment I sent a photo of the First Lady and me, which was taken during the reception for the National Design Award. I suppose I just wanted tell my strange new friend that she was messing with someone who knew an even more powerful woman with perfect biceps.

I bet you are dying to know if I ever received a response. I'll tell you on another occasion.

Rick Valicenti is the founder and design director of Thirst/3st, a communication design firm devoted to art, function, and real human presence. He has been influencing the design discourse internationally since 1988 and is a leading presence in design as a practitioner, educator, and mentor.

The White House honored Valicenti in 2011 with the Smithsonian Cooper-Hewitt, National Design Award for Communication Design. In 2006, he received the AIGA Medal, the highest honor of the graphic design profession, for his sustained contribution to design excellence and the development of the profession. Valicenti is a former president of the Society of Typographic Arts (STA) and is a member of the AGI (Alliance Graphique Internationale) since being invited in 1996. In 2004, he was recognized as a Fellow of the AIGA Chicago.

Over the past 30 years, Valicenti has publicly presented his work through lectures, workshops, and critiques on the design industry to more than 100 professional and college audiences on five continents. He has edited a 356-page monograph on the Thirst work titled, *Emotion as Promotion*, published in 2005 by the Monacelli Press.

Valicenti and Thirst's work is included in the permanent collection of the Cooper-Hewitt National Design Museum and the 2006 Triennial, Design Life Now, the Art Institute of Chicago, and the Library of the Museum of Modern Art. The work continues to advance the public design discourse while pushing the boundaries of graphic and intermedia design.

A good Irish toast

by Lana Rigsby

It was a lovely morning. Another perfect day for bicycling through pretty green countryside under cloudless blue skies. I groaned and pulled the covers over my head. I'd ridden my bike a hundred miles the day before, another hundred the day before that, sixty-five miles the day before that. My husband and I were with friends on a cycle-across-Ireland adventure and I was tired of it. All the fresh air and my friends' relentlessly good moods were wearing me out.

" In a tenor voice with a nearly impenetrable Irish brogue he began to sing: "I'm goin' down, down, down in a barn-in' ring o' fay-er" … "

The truth is I was pooped even before we'd started. Sad. Listless. John and I had been hoping for a baby and it wasn't working out. We'd thought the trip would be a welcome distraction for us both but that wasn't exactly happening either. I had no idea what would make me feel better, but I knew I wasn't finding it on my bike. So that day I called in sick. I feigned sniffles, waved off sympathy, and said goodbye as my companions flew off down the hill, gears clicking. When they were gone I wandered down the hill too.

It was still morning, brilliant and sunshiny. I headed straight for a pub.

I needn't have wondered whether the place would be open so early; it was. I stepped through the door and as my eyes adjusted to the dim light I felt the room go quiet.

A hoarse stage whisper broke the silence: "Good God, lads. There she is. The woman I shoulda married." A wizened man with twinkling eyes stepped toward me from the shadows and held out his hand. He looked to be at least 70 years old. In a tenor voice with a nearly impenetrable Irish brogue he began to sing: "I'm goin' down, down, down in a barn-in' ring o' fay-er" ...

My heart ballooned. A Johnny Cash song ... here? This guy somehow had my number! And suddenly I was exactly where I wanted to be. The thing I longed for was a simple good time—a day with nothing particular to do and some easy company. I remembered an Irish man I'd known in school, a sweet, beautiful fellow who told great stories and sang good songs and made me laugh. At least once, I knew that my friend took the day off work just to sit in the sun. I loved him for it. Irishmen get better with age, he'd told me, and looking around I got the feeling I'd stumbled on some that were as good as they get.

My suitor finished his serenade and took a bow, then sat down at a table where four men sat playing cards. He looked to be the youngest guy at the table. One man pulled a chair over for me and another dealt me in. The bartender drew a Guinness from the tap, velvety black with a thick creamy head, and set the glass aside for the long minutes it took the foam to settle. I eyed it while we played Twenty-Five. When at last the glass was set in front of me I lifted it and racked my brain for a toast. Nothing. But then I remembered where I was. "Teach me a toast!" I implored. "A good Irish toast."

The men looked at me with new interest. They cast sidelong glances at one another, rubbed their chins and looked at me again. "Oh, 'tis sure we know some, love."

"The trouble is, we've got no ale …" And sure enough, the table was bare except for cards. "A round for the gentlemen, please." I smiled. A barmaid drew the pints; I counted out Irish pounds. As the stout settled the men argued the merits of different toasts and decided on one in Gaelic.

"Sláinte go sail agat."

The table was covered with empty glasses before I'd mastered the first line to their satisfaction. This was a beautiful toast, they told me, a timeless blessing, and Gaelic a language so ancient God spoke it to Adam at the birth of the world. The toast must be said perfectly or not at all. Did I understand? Yes I did. But what does it mean? And what comes next? The men shook their heads and looked at their glasses mournfully. Of course! I ordered a round of Irish whiskies and laid my money down. They brightened, and taught me the second line: "Talamh gan cíos agat."

Before long my tongue began having trouble with the words; the pronunciation seemed to get progressively trickier. But the men, who clearly had all day, were patient. Over more Twenty-Five they told a string of the funniest stories I've ever heard and lectured me about picking up the kitty before naming my trump. They discussed the qualities that make Irish whiskey superior to Scotch. They told why toasts often end with a wish for "death in Ireland": Because during the Great Hunger a million displaced Irishmen lived only to go home. They showed dog-eared photos of kids and grandkids and asked me about babies and I said not yet—soon. Morning became afternoon before I had perfected the toast's last lines: "Leanbh gach blian agat. Gob fliuch, agus bás in Éirinn."

There. Done. Learnt. I wobbled unsteadily to my feet, lifted my glass, and said it all— articulating the phrases slowly, carefully. We celebrated with one last glass of the bar's best then I dumped the rest of my money onto the table and hugged the men goodbye.

I was weaving my way back up the hill when a woman's voice penetrated the buzzing in my ears: "Lay-dy! Ring o' fire lady! Wait, wouldya?" It was the barmaid from the pub. She labored up the lane after me and when she reached me, thrust a mountain of fragrant, booze-sodden bills into my hands. "The boys sent me to bring ya back yer money—they wounta never let you buy their drinks! They was a-pullin' your leg to hear you say the toast." I trailed Irish money all the way home and fell into bed, awakening just in time for dinner.

When I opened my eyes, the world looked different. Better. I told my story over dessert then stood and raised my glass one last time that day. In practically perfect Gaelic, I delivered a toast that translates something like this:

> "Health and long life to you, land without rent to you,
> a child every year to you, a wet mouth, and death in Ireland."

It's now many years later and I've said this little blessing at least a hundred times since then: no celebratory dinner, no Thanksgiving, no wedding or baby shower has been exempt from a recitation of The Toast. One day I'll teach it to Jack and Annie, the twins born to John and me two winters later and I know that, like me, they'll be grateful for its magic.

....

Lana Rigsby is a storyteller with a whiff of the seanchaí in her veins. Her stories range from the small but important ones she tells her kids to the big important ones her firm, Rigsby Hull, tells on behalf some of the world's most interesting companies. Lana was, and is, an avid cyclist.

The show must go on

by Scott Thares

Inspiration and life experiences are all around us. I tell students they should learn from any job experience, good or bad, and apply that knowledge to their own design sensibilities, regardless if it is even a design related job.

For example, maybe you develop a sense of brands and packaging design by

bagging groceries at your local supermarket. Perhaps selling clothes gives you a sense of fashion trends and consumer buying habits. Or maybe you develop and process film for the State Highway Patrol of drunk-driving fatalities—developing your color sense and even helping you understand how adjusting the CYMK levels really brings out the amount of blood and brains on the pavement. It might be long after you leave these jobs that you realize the profound effect they have on design thinking. All of these examples are jobs that I had at one point in time.

One job I had was a sea lion trainer. You might ask yourself, why a sea lion trainer, and where does one go to learn about training sea lions? The *why* was a no-brainer. How many people can put sea lion trainer on a business card? The days I spent with sea lions gave me stories for a lifetime. The *where* is a little less glamorous. One might think somewhere tropical and exotic like Hawaii or Mexico? No, it happened to be the Black Hills of South Dakota, not exactly tropical and definitely not exotic.

Before I could be hired at Marine Life Aquarium, my sea lion coworkers, aptly named Babes, BJ and Groucho, needed to feel comfortable in my presence. This marks the one and only time where animals needed to approve of me. Interestingly the names of these coworkers would be awesome names for dancers at gentlemen's clubs.

Over the next two weeks, I scrubbed, bathed, fed and worked performance routines with these new rubbery, fishy-smelling friends. Every pore and crevice on my body smelled like a fish market. I cut and prepared 75 pounds of halibut that was used as treats for training each day. These slimy chucks of halibut bait were placed in a bucket that was securely attached to my waist. I had to perfect hurling these chunks across the swimming pool into the mouths of each eager sea lion performer. These animals, though very wild, come across as big Great Danes. And like dogs, they are focused on one thing—food.

After my two-week trial run, I was ready for showtime in front of three hundred people. Outfitted with a wireless microphone, a rehearsed script and a bucket packed full of bait, I was ready! The show began with an introduction of each sea loin. From right to left on the swimming pool stage, I started with Groucho. He was the oldest of the performers and his name matched his personality. I mentioned he was rescued from a boating accident in California. When I finish his introduction and on cue, he barked in my face, the crowd chuckled and he got a treat. Next, it was on to BJ, I have no idea how he received that name but he was the teenager of the bunch. As I introduced him, he would blow me a kiss on my face, the crowd would laugh and I threw him a treat for reward.

I moved on to introduce the last performer, Babes. When I spoke to the audience I mentioned that he was the youngest and largest of the bunch. He weighs in at a hefty 600 pounds and he was close to 7' tall. By far, he was the most puppylike of the bunch. He was a lovable furless, giant baby bear. As I introduced Babes during my act, I place my hand on his shoulder and Babes put his flipper on my shoulder. The end result is that we looked like best friends, man and beast.

Except there was one problem: I reached out to put my hand on Babes and there was no Babes. No flipper on my shoulder.

Before I could determine where he was, his face was knee deep in my bait bucket. Did I mention the bucket was firmly attached to my waist?

Suddenly I went down, pulled to the ground, then dragged into the swimming pool below me.

Gasping for air before I was pulled under the water, I released the bait bucket from my waist. When I came back to the surface, I could see all three sea lions in the pool, barking and fighting over the bucket of food. The crowd at this point was in hysterics! Laughing and clapping, thinking that this was part of the show. Sadly, it was not. Meanwhile, I was trying desperately to get out of the pool. I did not want to get between the sea lions and their delight at an unexpected bonanza of halibut. This was unlike any traditional swimming pool at a public park. The edges of the pool were banked with a slow decline. The angle and wetness on the pool surface made it impossible for any human to get out, but easy for a sea lion with their large rubbery suctionlike flippers. I was struggling, slipping and sliding, trying to get free of my watery nightmare. Clawing at the sides of the pool did nothing. Here's a mental image, picture a kitten, soaking wet, that has fallen into a bathtub and is trying unsuccessfully to get out—and you'll have a pretty good idea of what I looked like. I made my way to a drainage pipe that was letting fresh water into the pool and finally pulled myself out.

Standing on solid ground, pumped full of adrenaline and sopping wet in front of an audience on their feet, clapping and laughing ... I politely took a bow. It was a great relief that I wasn't mauled to death.

As I gathered my wits, it took a moment to realize that my wireless mic was at the bottom of the pool. I was worried that one of the sea lions would mistake it for food and dove back into the pool to retrieve it. This erupted in more laughs and applause. As I crawled out of the pool for the second time, I was relieved yet again that I had escaped death by three sea lions circling the pool.

I raised my hand and walked off the stage as if I just finished an encore. It would have been an awesome "mic drop" had I been holding one. Though I may not of looked like a rock star, I felt a kinship with the likes of Paul Stanley that day.

Unfortunately, this was only five minutes of a forty-minute set. I still had to go back and finish the rest of the show. After almost being drowned, eaten alive and totally humiliated in front of a live audience, I went on to perform the show of a lifetime. This may have been the best damn sea lion show South Dakota has ever seen. Paul Stanley and the members of KISS would have loved to be in the audience that day. It definitely helped that I was quite relaxed (as I couldn't imagine it could possibly get any worse).

Looking back at my sea lion adventure, I realized how it has had a profound impact on me. It's my most retold story because really, how many people can say they trained sea lions? But, more importantly, it gave me the confidence to fail. To be embarrassed. To realize that when nothing is going as planned you have to find it in yourself to just keep going. This experience has given me the insight that when things go wrong and no matter how off the track work can get, take a deep breath, go back and do the a performance of a lifetime.

....

Scott Thares is creative director of Wink, an internationally recognized strategic brand design company that aspires to create solutions that impact both commerce and culture. The Minneapolis-based firm was named as one of the Style and Design 100 by *Time* magazine for their work with clients such as Target, Nike, MTV, Express, American Eagle Outfitters, Turner Classic Movies, JCPenney's, The Limited, Macy's, Neiman Marcus, Gaiam, Minnetonka Moccasin Co., and *The New York Times*. Work is included in the permanent collection of the Chicago Antheaum Museum, the Library of Congress, the Cooper Hewitt National Design Museum and has been featured on the best seller's list of *The New York Times*.

Never complain, never explain*

by Ann Willoughby

I have a reputation for a series of fashion faux pas spread over the last sixty years. In my case it was not always what I was wearing that was embarrassing.

It was my birthright to remain graceful and composed regardless of how embarrassing any situation might be. Growing up in Mississippi in the time of white gloves and pearls, being graceful and composed were de rigueur as a rite of passage—and this can be a problem, as you'll soon see.

I was four or five years old when I first noticed that people were amused at my ability to appear composed regardless of the circumstances.

For example, one day while playing in our garage, I found the little wooden potty chair I had used as a toddler. Don't ask me why, but I put my head all the way through the hole in the seat and my head became stuck. I ran to my mother and she was also unable to remove the chair.

So the two of us ("panicked Southern females") got in the car and drove for help. Imagine seeing a little girl in a 1946 Ford who was trying to appear like a little princess to other cars with a potty chair over her head. Meanwhile my mother was deciding whether to take me to a fire station, to an emergency room or to our family doctor. Because our doctor was just down the street, we went there. As I had anticipated and feared, the waiting room was full of other mothers with their kids. So like a proper little lady, I sat quietly and calmly next to my Mom waiting our turn while the other mothers and children found it impossible to stop giggling.

Another mishap happened in the eighth grade. One day, I wore a brand new crinoline petticoat to school that was made of multilayers and countless yards of stiff net and flounces of lace that made my skirt look like Scarlett O'Hara's hooped petticoat in the movie *Gone with the Wind*.

While chatting with friends in the parking lot after school, my crinoline petticoat was accidentally caught on the bumper of a car as the driver pulled away.

To everyone's amazement my crinoline unraveled in slow motion, yard by yard, layer by layer as the car disappeared around the corner with my white lace crinoline still attached to its bumper.

I slipped out of the remaining petticoat like nothing had happened while my friends guffawed loudly.

I won't even mention those high, high heels I wore in the 1960s. At 5'8" with 5" stilettos and a 5" beehive, I stood an impressive 6'6". No wonder boys didn't ask me out in high school.

And my reputation for humorous fashion faux pas has followed me into adulthood.

A few years ago I had an important meeting with a large corporate client to go over the contract for a new project we had been awarded. We had worked for months to win the business. I was supposed to call my new client's assistant from the corporate lobby and she was to come down and escort me to the meeting.

I was wearing a new pewter green Armani jacket and matching wide-leg trousers. Tres chic! As I approached the corporate entrance to the lobby I noticed something hanging out the bottom of my right trouser leg. It looked like a sock that had stuck to the inside of the right pant leg. Dang! So I discreetly did a bunny dip to release the sock.

The more I pulled, the more resistance there was. Finally a long pair of panty hose came flying out with such force that they flew into the air like a loaded slingshot. Somewhat flabbergasted by the trick pantyhose, I quickly regained my composure and stuffed the panty-hose in my handbag. When I reached the door about 6 feet away I realized my client was standing there and had seen everything.

Ann Willoughby is the founder, president and chief creative director of Willoughby Design—a brand innovation and identity design firm established in 1978. Willoughby has developed brand identities and campaigns for United Nation's Deliver Now, Kauffman Labs, Park Place Development, Noodles & Co., SPIN! Neapolitan Pizza, Feng, Lee Jeans, Hallmark Cards, Hershey's and Blue Valley CAPS School (Center for Advanced Professional Studies).

Ever active with AIGA, the professional association for design, Willoughby served on the National Board of Directors and in 2006 was named Kansas City's first national AIGA Fellow. Ann is a designer, illustrator, international speaker, design judge, teacher and writer. She helped launch the pilot AIGA design leadership program at Harvard and the Aspen Design Summit in Colorado. Willoughby was named one of the Top 20 International Identity Designers in the 2009 book *Masters of Design*. As a charter member of the Designer's Accord, a founding board member of the AIGA Center for Sustainable Design, and an ambassador for the Living Principles, Ann has become an acknowledged expert in sustainable design. In 2012, Ann was named the JC Hall Distinguished Professor of Design at the Kansas City Art Institute. Currently Ann cochairs the 2014 AIGA National Centennial Celebration.

Today, Willoughby brings her experience to companies on the forefront of entrepreneurial and business innovation.

Brazilian legends

by Matteo Bologna

"Dude, I can't see shit in this sewer."

"Really? Cause that's *all* I can see."

"Okay, okay, please stop complaining. I admit this wasn't my best idea."

"I can't believe I followed you down here. What a fucking idiot. How the fuck could this be a shortcut to Harlem?"

"Wow, it really stinks down here; what is that?"

"We are swimming up to our fucking knees in diarrhea; take a stab at what it might be."

"No, I'm pretty sure this is the right way. Just up here around this bend then it's pretty much plain sailing."

"If you say 'plain sailing' one more time I swear to God I will punch you in the face until you die. We are so far from fucking plain sailing right now I can't even ..." [Plop]

"Whoops."

"Holy fuck! You can't even hold onto a fucking torch!? Are you fucking kidding me!? *Now* I can't see shit. It's in my hair, it's in my ears and my shoes are full of it, but at least now I can't see it. Fuck. Me. No, fuck *you*."

"Don't freak out. Look, I'm fishing it out. I know exactly where it fell. Here I go. Look, it's here!"

"You're such a fucking genius. I do not believe that for a second."

"Nope, nope, I got it ... I got it ... "

"Why is this shit stream now moving?"

"ARGH! ARGH! HELP ME! ARGH! IT'S GOT MY HAND! ARGH. GET THIS THING OFF ME!! HELP, IT'S FUCKING TAKING ME UNDER. HANS, HELP ME!!"

"Fuck. Oh, fuck. Holy shit, Jorge. Your hand, it's gone! I think it's one of those albino killer crocodiles everyone's always talking about. I guess it's not bullshit. Wow, this is some fucked-up shit."

What you just read is a pretty accurate retelling of a true story I thought I'd share with you. It happened to a couple of friends of mine on their way home from a party one night. The victim's name isn't Jorge. I changed that detail to protect his privacy and reputation—but for those of you who are familiar with the graphic designer who has a hook, you can probably guess his true identity. And you have my permission to tell this story and say that you know the guy who knew the guys.

It may sound a tad sadistic, but this story actually makes me very happy. I've always loved the urban legend about the crocodiles that live deep beneath the streets of New York, swimming through the sewers, eating shit and growing to Jurassic proportions. Apparently their existence was the result of vacationing New Yorkers who transported baby crocodiles back from Florida to keep as pets, then once the animals started to get big and tried biting their limbs off, they got

"

The victim's name isn't Jorge. I changed that detail to protect his privacy and reputation—but for those of you who are familiar with the graphic designer who has a hook, you can probably guess his true identity.

"

scared and flushed them down the toilet. This piece of New York folk-lore is made all the more cool by the fact that these feces-loving beasts are also slightly stoned as they meander through sewers in the dark, their high a result of all the marijuana baggies that are flushed down the city's toilets during drug raids. This is what would make NYC the city I always imagined: Streets that smell like some stealth, lurking, shit-drenched predator, not like Hollister and waxed ball-sacks and frappuccinos. If this were true I could tell my friends in Italy that I live and survive in New York, and they would consider me cool. And manly. Instead I shop at Zara and so do they.

This isn't my only brush with urban legend, I'd like you to know. There's the story of my elephantine manhood (okay, so I started that one myself), but to date no one else has gone on the record to help perpetuate that rumor. And then there's the story of the time I vacationed to Brazil. When people meet me today, fifteen years after the trip in question, they still eye me pathetically, like I'd just flashed them my superfluous nipple, and say, "Wow! You're that guy?" I guess that's because most travel mishaps involve turning up at an un-booked hotel or telling the cabdriver the wrong airport terminal. Not many people fly to the wrong country. But yep, I'm that guy. I think it was some old dead American who said that life is about the journey not the destination. Or, actually, no, it was Steven Tyler and Aeros-mith. Anyway, for me, the journey sucked and the destination was the wrong place, so I managed to get fucked both ways. Not always easy on a family vacation.

Back in the mid-1990s, in an era where human beings still used travel agents to book flights, myself and the former Mrs. Bologna, after working our asses off for a couple of years without a real vacation, decided to travel to our dream destination: Brazil. More precisely Sal-vador de Bahia: the capital of Salvador, one of the biggest states of the magnificent country which gave us samba and bossa nova; the home-town of Caetano Veloso and Gilberto Gil, and where they founded the Tropicália movement in the late 1960s; but more important, a place with sand and an ocean and a million miles away from the noise and stress of Manhattan. Cristina (the ex), who always liked to organize trips, called her usual travel agent to arrange our tickets—he is her phone pal, the guy who books her flights to India, where she goes many times a year for work. After regaling her for several minutes about the natural beauty of Brazil, he searched for deals and found a flight that is much less than the regular fare. It's not direct, but hey, it's half price, so she takes it.

Fast forward to the day of the trip. It's 5 A.M., and I delivered the last stroke of a job just three hours earlier. But it doesn't matter that I'm tired as shit—I'm finished, packed and ready to fly. Sun and sand, here I come. As I'm sitting on my connecting flight awaiting takeoff, I adjust the time of my wristwatch to our destination. We have a little quarrel about Brazil's time zone, which still remains a mystery to us, even after our agreement that it is probably a couple of hours ahead of NYC time. Then an announcement comes through the plane's PA system. We'd only recently moved to New York from Italy and understood about 70 percent of what was spoken to us by American speakers— and British-English is worth another chapter, suffice to say that I still watch *Downton Abbey* with subtitles.

After the announcement I realize that British-English is not the only English outside of my comprehension repertoire. Now Airplane-Speaker-English is added to the list of language variations I need to master. I grasped that the first part of the announcement relates to the length of the flight (I guess somewhere between four to fourteen hours, give or take), the use of electronics is permitted (I can finally use my new portable CD player!) and the local time and destination (Salvador). However, the second part of the announcement puzzles me.

....

I'm a longtime lover of Brazilian music, therefore pretty familiar with the sound of Brazilian-Portuguese, but the announcement seems to be given in Spanish.

....

Not Brazilian-Spanish (which I know for sure does not exist), but Spanish-Spanish. I continue to wonder why Delta Airlines would deliver a message in a language different from that of the country of destination, and as the plane begins to pick up speed and heads down the runway, I look around uselessly for a few clues. But none of my fellow passengers seem to be sipping caipirinhas or strumming guitars. I tried to express my doubts to my sleepy companion but she dismissed me with a wave as she drifted off to Morpheus world. Thinking I must have had auditory hallucinations, I return to my Lonely Planet guide to Brazil. I read about all the scary things that can happen to a tourist whose demeanor is too much like that of a tourist. Apparently local thieves love to smear visitors with water (or pee or even feces) and when somebody arrives to help you clean your clothes, they also clean you of your valuables. Following the guide's instructions, I promptly begin disguising myself as a native by taking off my watch and earrings. (In reality I never wore ear-rings, but this is my story and it's set in the 1990s, so I'd like you to imagine me as the type of guy who could've pulled off big studs in each ear.) Soon lunch arrives and there is a choice of chicken or pasta—or more correctly, pollo or pasta. Pollo?!! That is not Portuguese, is it?

The nagging doubt that I'm on the wrong plane now starts to take seed. Despite being inappropriate and verbally filter-free, I am naturally quite shy, and I don't like to ask stupid questions in fear of being judged. So I avoid asking the flight attendant the glaring question in fear of the two obvious responses I may receive: I played out both scenarios in my mind: "Yes, Mr. Bologna, you are indeed on the wrong plane. And yes, you are indeed a fucking idiot." Or: "You think our airline is going to board passengers on the wrong flight? Mr. Bologna, you really are a fucking idiot."

So guided by my lack of balls, I devise the perfect solution to my burning question: checking the in-flight magazine to see which movie is shown on the leg from Atlanta to Salvador de Bahia. Jack-pot! *Analyze This* is playing on the plane monitors, and it is also listed in the movie guide for my flight to Brazil! Phew, I'm such an idiot. Rookie traveler. How can I possibly think that I can be on the wrong plane when the ticket plainly says NYC to San Salvador? I think that's what the ticket says.

Everything is fine now. I'm relaxing with Robert De Niro who is being analyzed by Billy Crystal, and I am sipping crappy airplane drinks in plastic cups while picturing myself in South American sands drinking tropical cocktails and being massaged with coconut oil. Then comes the landing announcements. Did they say "Asegurar cuerdas de sillón"? "Aterrizaje." Is that really Portuguese? My ex finally awakes, puzzled, and gives me a look that says: "Usually you are an idiot, but I'll put aside spousal biases and years of jetting around the world to think that you might be onto something."

Finally we part the plane and are saluted by a welcome crew with a definitely non-Portuguese, "Buena vacation, señores!" In truth, it feels we are walking to the gallows with no idea in which country we are about to be hung. And also, do I need a visa to die here? Apparently I do not, because this is not death row. According to the stamp on my passport it's just El Salvador. Cristina does not believe it. It is not possible. She was on the phone with the fucking agent for twenty minutes talking about the majesty of Brazil. How can he have given us tickets for the wrong fucking country? So to bring her to reality I give her a $20 bill and send her to the Banquo to exchange it into local currency. She exits the facility with a dazed expression and a plastic bag filled with bills stamped with the picture of some general who probably liberated the country from some colonialist asshole making it a free REPÚBLICA DE EL SALVADOR.

I didn't know whether to blame it on the bossa nova, my wife or the fucking travel agent from Destinations Are Not Us. All I know is that this is not the Brazil of my sunset dreams. Not to be superficial, but I was looking forward to all of those athletic, waxed, tanned Brazilians in butt-floss bikinis. The people milling outside this airport were, shorter, hairier and more fully clothed than what I had in mind. Less pro beach-volleyball match, more busboy convention.

What does the guide for the intrepid traveler say to do in this situation? I have no fucking idea. First, because I do not have that manual; second, because this situation should not happen; and third, because I'm a leisure traveler. I hate adventure. In my life everything needs to be planned months in advance to maximize the enjoyment of doing absolutely nothing (i.e., designing typefaces without interruption) during my holiday stay. I tell my wife to, "Keep calm, let's not panic. Let's plan a solution: What do we know about a country for which we have not a travel guide?" We confer and the only two bits of information we know about El Salvador is that the country is somewhere in Central America and possibly in the midst of civil war. As in the plane, I am afraid to ask anybody: "Excuse me señor: Are you still slaughtering each other in the street, or are you back friendly with your neighbor?" (Remember, this was during the dark ages of pre–World Wide Web.)

Being that this is nonfiction, the rest of the story is kind of anticlimactic. We didn't get shot at, strung up or, sadly, smeared with Brazilian feces. Seeing that there were no flights to the Salvador of our intentions, and because it was impossible to find a tourist guide for the country anywhere, we ended up traveling blindly for the rest of the week.

One good thing: We figured out with relief that the war ended more or less a couple of years prior to our trip.

So now you can name that friend of a friend, and I give you my blessing to spread this tale of extreme idiocy—my street credibility is so solid (cough) I feel secure that my intellectual reputation shall remain unsoiled. In case you're wondering why I told you previously about the sewer mishap of Jorge and Hans: it's because I feel that we embarked on a similar journey. The only difference is that they actually ended up in Harlem. And Jorge may be missing a foot (I lied, it wasn't a hand). But just as sad as poor Jorge's plight, I've still never managed to set my own feet in Brazil.

Matteo Bologna is the founding partner and principal of Mucca Design, where he also serves as creative director.

Under his direction, the Mucca Design team has solved numerous design challenges and created uniquely successful work for a wide variety of companies, among them Victoria's Secret, André Balazs Properties, Barnes & Noble, Rizzoli, Starr Restaurants, Patina Restaurant Group, Adobe Systems and Target.

The work produced by the Mucca Design team has been widely recognized by industry publications, competitions and exhibitions including: AIGA, *Communication Arts, Eye, Graphis, HOW, Print, STEP*, the Art Directors Club, the James Beard Foundation, and the Type Directors Club.

Matteo is the vice president of the Type Directors Club. He frequently lectures about branding and typography around the world.

The importance of trophies

by Chris Hill (as told to Mike Hicks)

On a holiday weekend many years ago, I was visiting my parents in Bonham, Texas. It's the small town where I grew up quite happily playing football, running track and sneaking an occasional beer with friends.

I was an Eagle Scout simply as a matter of course. It was as natural and fully expected as a third down off-side rush. My dad sold life insurance to just about everyone in town while my mother tended to me and my sisters, cooked conventional meals and decorated competitively with friends from her bridge club.

On this particular Saturday, I kept Dad company during his weekend morning ritual of drinking coffee while reading *The Bonham Daily Favorite* and watching television news. It occurred to me, sitting there in the den, that this was the perfect time to bring him up to speed about my career and recent accomplishments. Though very supportive, my parents had about as much of an idea about my professional career as I did about their sex life. (In that regard, less is more had always been my motto, and I was quite content to believe my siblings and I were the result of Immaculate Conception.)

The world I was living and working in was far removed from the sleepy town of Bonham. After graduating from college, I ended up in Houston at a high-profile design firm. Six years later, I went into business for myself. It was fun, and my firm was prospering, with national and international clients and a growing reputation in New York, Los Angeles and Tokyo. In Bonham, Texas, however, there was not a single individual who could conceive of money being exchanged for what I did, assuming they had any idea of what, in fact,

I did. Therefore it seemed only right, sitting in my dad's den, that I should at least let him in on it. I wanted him to know how accomplished I was at my profession.

So during a station break and coffee refill, I started talking, nervously at first, I worked my way to a complete and glowing review of my career thus far. Achieving full steam, I boasted of having my work in the permanent collection of the Museum of Modern Art in New York and in the archives of the Library of Congress and having won not one, but two gold medals in the Art Directors Club of New York show. "It's sort of like winning an Oscar, Dad, or an Emmy," I explained.

With his newspaper in his lap, he sipped his coffee, smiled and said, "Do you remember going to the bowling alley with me when I was in the league?"

"Yes," I replied, trying desperately to figure out what this could possibly have to do with the conversation thus far.

"Remember when our team won the big tournament and I brought home that trophy?"

"Sure, Dad," I said, wondering if this was one of the symptoms of early dementia I should have noticed earlier.

"Well, the next day I went over to the barbershop for some coffee," he continued. (The town's barbershop was the equivalent of Starbucks and the social center of Bonham.) "I told all the fellows there that I'd won the tournament trophy, and everyone congratulated me."

"That's great, Dad, but ..."

"Here's my point, son," he soldiered on, "after all the congratulations, nobody said another thing about it. We talked about the weather, old Mr. Wilson's funeral, beef prices, but not another word was spoken about the tournament or my trophy. You see, they were sincerely happy for me, but they weren't in the tournament. So it really didn't mean a damned thing to them."

I must have looked utterly confused at that point, because he couldn't quite hide the smile behind his coffee cup.

"Your mother and I are real proud of you and your accomplishments son," he said, suddenly serious, "and it's gratifying to win awards and the respect of your peers.

"But never forget: to everyone else those awards and honors are just so many bowling trophies. No better. No worse."

My confusion turned to chagrin as I realized he was trying to let me down gently. Then he got out of his chair, hugged me and murmured, "We love you Chris. It makes us happy that you're happy. That's all that's important to us."

Needless to say, it was one of the more humbling experiences of my life, but nonetheless strangely uplifting. A few years later, I shared this story while speaking to an AIGA chapter in Minneapolis. After the talk, Eric Madsen, an old friend from Texas, and I went out for drinks to catch up with one another. He told me how much he liked the bowling trophy story and wanted to know more about my dad. Later in the evening, I quipped to Eric, "Well, I still haven't been featured in *CA* [*Communication Arts*], but I don't think they're losing much sleep over it in Bonham." He agreed it was most likely not in their top ten list of countywide disappointments.

Though I joked about it often, having The Hill Group featured in *CA* magazine was, in fact, my number one professional goal. It always had been. I still remember the day a few years later when our receptionist told me some guy named Dick Coyne was on the phone wanting to talk to me. I tried to feign surprise, but I'd been waiting on his call for fifteen years. It was all I could do not to blurt out, "Finally!" At long last my feature article had arrived.

A week or so after the magazine came out, I was still reveling in my newfound fame when I noticed a large box sitting in the reception area addressed to me. I lugged it back to my office and discovered it was from Eric in Minneapolis. Inside I found a magnificent bowling trophy ornately adorned with golden angels wrapped in fake snakeskin and crowned by the inevitable 24K bowler. On its base was engraved:

Chris Hill—The Hill Group
Communication Arts Magazine
1st Place—1994

CHRIS HILL — THE HILL GROUP
COMMUNICATION ARTS MAGAZINE
1st PLACE – 1994

Though Dad had passed away several years earlier, I instantly thought of him and realized he, of all people, would have smiled in understanding at such a gift. Today the trophy remains proudly beside my desk, constantly reminding me of my family, my friends and what's truly important in life. Thanks Dad, and thanks Eric.

....

For the last 33 years, Chris Hill has been president and creative director of HILL, an internationally recognized branding firm in Houston, Texas.

HILL delivers branding and marketing solutions to high-profile clients both in the United States and abroad.

HILL's work has been featured in most major design competitions in the United States, as well as many foreign competitions, and is included in the permanent collections of the Ellis Island/Statue of Liberty Commemorative Exhibit, the Museum of Modern Art in New York City, the National Collection of Modern and Contemporary Arts in Munich, Germany, and the Library of Congress American Graphic Art Collection in Washington, DC.

Chris Hill received the American Institute of Graphic Arts Fellow Award for his lifetime of achievement in the graphic design community and arts education. Chris taught on weekends at Texas State University for 15 years, which inspired him to organize and host the Creative Summit, a nationally recognized annual creative conference and student competition, which is now celebrating its 28th year. The Creative Summit brings top professionals from all parts of the creative industry to speak and judge student portfolios. Over the last five years over $100,000 cash scholarships have been awarded to outstanding student work.

School is out

by Yang Kim

I've had waves of employees over the years, and many of the same issues seem to come up again and again.

There's one that I think is especially interesting: Some people can't help talking badly about difficult clients.

Once you label someone, they become that person for you. He's the Sleep-On-It Guy, or she's Ms. Win-Win. Or worse, you get into less inventive name-calling.

It's true that we have had our share of difficult clients. Who hasn't? And it's tempting to label them. When I need to summon a little willpower to resist, I think back to one particular instance.

This client was really awful. He talked big but always had to check in with the boss. He never missed an opportunity to flaunt that his office was in Manhattan or that his company had offices across the country. He was in charge of the purse strings, and we were to remember that. When it came to direction, he was the type of client who liked to say, "I'll know it when I see it," and he'd often talk down to our designers and ask not-very-helpful questions like, "Why aren't you picking the right images?" You get the picture.

Well, one day he mentioned—apropos of nothing, other than to hold one over me—that he had attended an Ivy League school.

I'm all for education, but at some point, it doesn't matter.

If you're brilliant, then you're brilliant. Once you hit forty, there's twenty years of distance between you and your undergrad days. Have the intervening decades been so uneventful that a twenty-year-old degree is your primary source of validation?

What he didn't know—and I never mentioned to him—was the fact that I was actually accepted to an Ivy League school (Harvard) but didn't go. It wasn't right for me at the time looking for a degree in design. Years later, I also participated in Harvard's executive education program. I suppose that does sound a little impressive.

When I shared this story with a colleague who also had experience working with this particular person, he offered some wisdom from his long-time mentor who had faced a similar situation. My colleague's mentor told him, "Honey, the world is run by C students, so get used to it."

With a long list of design awards to her name, Yang Kim has made a mark on contemporary graphic design. Much acclaim has resulted from her fruitful collaboration with Herman Miller's chief creative officer Stephen Frykholm on the last ten of the company's killer annual reports. Yang has had vast experience in designing everything from complex corporate product literature programs to fun, little holiday cards. While leading Peopledesign, her fifteen-year-old design firm, Yang continues to design, direct and manage projects of all kinds and sizes. In 2011, Peopledesign was recognized by *Inc.* magazine as one of the fastest growing private companies in America.

Yang's work has been recognized by major design competitions including the New York Art Directors Club, the Type Directors Club of New York, *Communication Arts, Critique*, the American Institute of Graphic Art, *Graphis, HOW, ID (International Design)*, the Mead Annual Report Show, *Print, AR100* and *Creativity*. In 2011, Yang received the Silver Medal Award, the highest honor given by American Advertising Federation chapters. It's an award her mentor, Steve Frykholm, whose Herman Miller posters hang in museums around the world, received just two years prior. Yang has been recognized as one of West Michigan's 50 Most Influential Women and by Inforum's Inner Circle, an honor representing a variety of the region's most accomplished professional women.

Dancing with tears in my eyes

by Marc Atlan

In 1991, the late famous designer, Madame Andrée Putman (1925–2013), was throwing a lavish party to celebrate the moving of her furniture company, Écart International.

I had been a longtime and fervent admirer of her work. Since I was just out of design school, in my early twenties and not connected to her world, I had not been invited to the event. My naive determination led me to a decision to force my way in to the party, and miraculously I managed to do just that.

Ultimately I had an ulterior motive beyond getting free food and drinks. A couple of weeks before, at another design event, I had been magnetically attracted to the sight of a beautiful stranger. The event was aptly titled Pour La Vie. While walking into the only restroom at this opening, the most beautiful woman I had ever seen was just walking out.

We locked eyes.

For a long time.

She gave me a long charming smile.

I was immediately and definitively caught under her spell.

My crashing of Andrée Putman's party was basically an excuse—or more precisely an attempt—at potentially seeing this woman again.

While "Le tout Paris" was mingling, I managed to find Christian Ghion—a very good friend of mine—and we started discussing life. One of the subjects was this mysterious woman. In his typical "rough around the edges yet teddy bear" manner, my friend Christian bluntly told me to not overread her smile, that he knew of her, that she was working for another famous design company and that basically "It was her job to smile."

I was absolutely infuriated by his demeaning comment, which was unacceptable to me, both in terms of why this woman had such a pleasant approach to life and also because I saw it as a lame attempt to crush my chances of potentially approaching the woman of my dreams.

Suddenly, this woman came into my view. She saw me from across the room and unequivocally smiled again.

Renewed hope.

Rush of adrenaline.

Instant passion.

I decided to make a bet with my friend.

The bet went as follows: I would have to find a way to approach and invite Madame Andrée Putman—the famous host of the party— to dance with me in front of "Le tout Paris."

Christian asserted that my chances were close to zero, nada, zilch. Andrée was surrounded by an army of VIPs—such as her friend Didier Grumbach, president of the Parisian Haute Couture Federation and one of the most powerful and intimidating men in Paris—and a legion of important celebrities and chatty socialites. Christian was unfortunately quite right. The chances of getting close to Andrée Putman—let alone asking her to dance with me!— seemed like mission impossible.

I downed a flute of champagne, and another one, and another one. I made sure that my beautiful stranger was looking in my direction, took a deep breath and made my move. To this day, I remember my friend's hand grabbing my arm and his voice telling me, "Don't you dare Atlan. It is guaranteed humiliation!"

Fuck it. Fuck him. I had to win my bet, and most important, I had to make a bold move to impress this woman.

I fiercely walked towards Madame Putman—who was standing midway up a beautiful staircase, surrounded by Parisian leeches and

"

The bet went as follows: I would have to find a way to approach and invite Madame Andrée Putman—the famous host of the party—to dance with me in front of "Le tout Paris."

"

self-important wannabes—and finally ended up on this staircase, two steps below Andrée Putman, looking up at my hero.

Showtime!

While blood was rushing through my veins—almost in a dream-like state—I heard myself saying: "Madame Putman?"

Her fascinating face turned towards me, and in her recognizable raspy voice, she elegantly replied: "Yes, young man, what can I do for you?"

"Well, Madame Putman, I simply wanted to tell you that you have in front of you the most passionate admirer of your work."

"What a delightful comment. Your genuineness is incontestable. Thank you!"

"Madame, I would not want to overstep my boundaries, but I have a huge favor to ask of you."

"You can always ask."

"Well, the music seems to fill this space, but nobody is dancing. Would you please give me the pleasure of accepting to dance with me?"

Five very long seconds went by.

Heart pounding.

Emotional liquefaction inside.

Trying to stay composed on the outside.

"My dear young man, you have no idea *how long* it has been since a handsome man has asked me to dance. *You* are doing me a favor. Thank you, and I gladly accept!"

Big smiles.

Quick glance at my stranger. Was she looking at me? Yes!

Tradition oblige, I took Madame Andrée Putman's arm, and walked her down the staircase.

I literally could feel a thousand eyes on us.

Nobody was dancing.

I took Madame Putman's left hand, placed my right arm against her lower back.

"Shall we?"

"Ab-so-lu-te-ly, young man!"

And there I was, teary-eyed, dancing with my hero, my star.

After the song ended, Madame Putman profusely thanked me and told me it felt good to be treated like a woman, that she should do this more often and politely excused herself to return to her guests.

I thanked her in return, told her it had been a privilege and that I would never forget this magical moment.

She kissed me goodbye, left and suddenly the dance floor was stormed by all her guests.

My body felt drained yet so alive!

I found my friend Christian in the crowd.

"Atlan, you have testicular titanium! I simply can't believe what I just witnessed..."

"Christian, I believe you owe me one!"

"Well, Atlan, you have serious cojones, but you forgot to set the reward for our bet, so it's a draw."

"Seriously man? You're killing me! Oh well, I guess the prize was the dance anyway."

Later on, I found even more renewed courage and went to talk to my beautiful stranger. She told me she was quite impressed by what I just did in front of this imposing crowd. We talked, smiled (apparently not her job, Christian), flirted and agreed to see each other very soon.

Andrée will always be my lucky charm, my guardian angel.

Twenty-two years later, I am still married to my beautiful stranger.

"Pour la Vie" indeed.

....

Marc Atlan is a French-born American Creative Director based in Los Angeles, California. He conceptualizes and designs perfume bottles and packagings, ad campaigns and catalogues, logos and brand identities, magazine designs as well as store displays, events, installations and TV commercials.

His diverse roster of clients features Comme des Garçons, Helmut Lang, Tom Ford, Yves Saint Laurent, Prada Beauty, Marc Jacobs, Maison Martin Margiela, Cartier, Capitol Records, Oliver Stone, Joe Pytka, Philippe Starck, Coty Prestige, and Christian Dior Couture & Parfums. His current creations include projects for David Beckham, H&M and the Dennis Hopper Art Trust.

For more than two decades, Marc Atlan has been recognized internationally by more than forty awards including winning a Red Dot, a Gold Pentaward, a Gold One Show, Best Packaging of the year by *I.D.* magazine and has received a Best Packaging Design recognition at the european FiFi Awards.

Marc Atlan was honored by having his work selected as a Top 10 Design of the Year by *Time* magazine, as well as a Top 5 Design of the Year by *Wallpaper* magazine. He has recently been awarded the prestigious Product Designer of the Year title by the Pacific Design Center in their "Stars of Design" awards ceremony.

Recently, Marc notably originated the idea of teaming up David Beckham with H&M, art directed the packagings, billboards and worldwide ad campaign and became responsible for "one of the most talked about Super Bowl TV commercials ever aired" (Source: Ad Age®, Super Bowl XLVI). The following season, in a bold move, Atlan selected Guy Ritchie as the movie director who would shoot the upcoming Spring 2013 TV Commercial based on Marc's original concept and script.

On burning up

by Jeff Greenspan

 Back in the late 1990s I lived in San Francisco. My apartment was at the top of Nob Hill, and it had a roof with views that allowed you to easily see both the Bay Bridge and the Golden Gate.

Given the amazing views, many of us in the building kept grills up there for BBQs.

One day I went up there with my buddy Jason Stanfield to make some burgers. I was shocked by what I saw—or, I should say, by what I didn't see. My grill was gone. Not just my grill but everybody's grill. There were no grills for as far as the eye could see, and on clear evening like that one, that was as far as Alcatraz.

I freaked out. I really went nuts. I was so angry someone would take *my stuff*. I took it as a personal affront. Such reactions were one of my big issues—as were making things all about me and expressing runaway anger. Okay, that's more than one issue, but back to me.

Jason calmly tried to explain that since everybody's grill was gone, having the grills up there probably violated a rule of the building. And, in any event, it was just a $40 grill, nothing worth getting all riled up about. I wasn't having any of that. The foghorns off of Fisherman's Wharf punctuated my rooftop screaming as I eventually tired myself out with anger.

The next day my landlady told the tenants the fire marshal was doing an inspection and that she had hid all our grills so the building wouldn't get ticketed. We were free to have them back now that the coast was clear.

After that incident Jason would use the say the word *grill* to remind me to stay calm and not let anger get the best of me, especially when I may not have all the facts.

Years later, once Jason and I moved to different cities, *grill* was still a constant companion. I'd say it to myself over and over whenever I felt a raging fit coming on.

Photo: U-Shin Kim

I repeated it in my mind like a meditative mantra when the tailor, after being asked to fix my torn coat pocket, simply sewed it shut. "Grill. Grill."

It also came in handy during an American Airlines flight from LaGuardia to Atlanta. After spending three hours stuck on the tarmac, we were told to deplane and wait for a new aircraft and crew to arrive. A few more hours had passed and it was nearing 4 p.m. I'm was still in the LaGuardia's Terminal 5 and I approached the ticket agent to ask when my flight might be taking off.

She barely looked up from her keyboard. "Your flight is scheduled to leave at 4 P.M., sir"

Tired, hungry, and confused, I double-checked the time on my phone. "But it's a few minutes to four right now."

"That's right. Yes." She finally looked up, shooting me a boilerplate smile.

"So the new plane and crew are here?" I was hopeful but knew I shouldn't be.

"Oh, no sir, I'm not sure when your plane will be here." Her smile was as firmly stuck on her face as I was in the terminal.

"Gr—" I couldn't even complete the word in my head. "Gr—" I should have tried harder. *Gr—* It was only one syllable damn it. I was losing it. I was sure I was about to make it onto a no-fly list.

My hands shook. My left eye twitched. My voice became loud. "How can a plane that isn't even here, and a crew that isn't even here, be taking off in a few minutes? I just want to know if I have enough time to get some food!"

"Well, you're scheduled to depart at 4 P.M. sir, that's all I can tell you."

I gathered my luggage. "Have you ever heard of Kafka?"

Her smile vanished. "No, sir."

"Well, you should have, because you're in one of his realities." I turned and walked away, pleased that I had made the guy behind me laugh.

A few minutes later, the agent approached me in another part of the terminal. She was accompanied by someone who I'd soon learn was her supervisor. While the agent stood glaring at me with arms crossed in front of her, the supervisor asked for my ID and boarding pass.

"I understand you called this agent an offensive word."

I took a step backward, confused and angry. "What? No. I didn't."

The agent uncrossed her arms and pointed at me. "He called me a Kafka!"

I explained how Kafka was a literary giant who detailed how circular logic and bureaucratic nonsense crushed the human spirit. I connected the dots between a nonexistent plane taking off in five minutes and the utter feeling of alienation Kafka was able to express. The whole while my blood boiled and my head pounded.

Finally, the supervisor handed back my boarding pass and told me to be more careful next time. As they both walked away, "GRILL" came pouring out of my mouth, just beneath a yell. They looked back at me, confused, then went back to their keyboards.

Grill, I'm sure, kept me out of jail recently. I was sitting in a restaurant by myself. The tables in this place were very close together, and I was sitting next to a couple who appeared to be on their first or second date.

"So, when's your birthday?" I overheard the guy ask the woman he was with.

She thought about it a moment and sighed. "Ya know, I don't think I really have a birthday, because I was a C-section. So, like, I have a day when I was ripped out. But I don't know when I was supposed to be born. I mean, like, that would be my real birthday, but I don't know when that would have been. I mean, supposedly I'm an Aquarius, but maybe I'm really a Pisces. I'll never know."

....

My first instinct was to reach for my fork and stab her repeatedly in the face. "Grill. Grill. Grill."

....

And just like that, my hand unclenched and the fork dropped back to the table. It's hard to know for sure if any jury would have convicted me had I explained what I had heard. But *grill* certainly kept me from having to find out.

Years later I moved back to back to New York City. I found an apartment at 2nd and B, and the view from my living room window included none other than the word GRILL in huge red neon letters. It was the partially obscured signage from a bar/restaurant across the

street, and it perfectly framed the word that had come to be such a help to me. It served as a good, constant reminder to not let the world get to me. Which is real easy to forget in a city like New York, which I still live in today. Thanks, Jace.

Jeff Greenspan is the chief creative officer at BuzzFeed where he oversees BuzzFeed Labs, an experimental arm of the social media company that's creating new ways for the internet to enjoy the internet. During his free time he performs improv comedy and launches personal projects like SelflessPortraits. com, New York City's Tourist Lanes, and Hipster Traps. He also plays chess, snaps pictures on the streets, and enjoys art and design. He's paid rent in San Francisco, Los Angeles, and London, but currently resides in New York City's West Village and online at www.jeffgreenspan.com.

Tercio de muerte

by Christopher Simmons

From Barcelona the train will take four hours. Packed with sunburnt Aussies and Americans in unwashed clothes. Men mostly. Fucking animals. Drinking and boasting and shoving each other down the cramped aisle.

Tomorrow one of them will climb to the top of a monument and, before jumping into the twisted thicket of waiting arms, will piss on the crowd below. He'll die when they don't catch him. "What did he expect would happen?"1 That's what someone will say to me. When I ask if he knew the man who died the stranger will answer no (he'll answer yes when I ask if that's the man's blood on his shirt). You killed him you know—I'll say—not you, but all of you. You killed him because he pissed on you. He'll ask again, "What did he think would happen when he pissed on us?" When I reply I'll stress the pronoun: What did you think would happen when you didn't catch him? The stranger will walk away.

In Pamplona my brother will run with the bulls (well, *from* them, really) but I won't. We'll sleep in the common hallway on the second floor of an apartment building until someone kicks us out, then find a dewy slope in the park and curl up with our wallets and passports down the front of our pants. Later, at the bullfight, half of the stadium will be in shadow while the sol seats broil in the sun. Everyone wears white to watch a black bull die. In the stands, men will splash sangria on the passing women until their blouses cling to their breasts and run red with the stain of sweet wine. (A bullfighter's cape is red to hide the blood.)

At the end of his seduction it will be our half—the scorched half—that pelts the matador with fruit and bottles when he fails both the *estocada* and the *descabello*. Yes, now we judge him. After the third unsuccessful thrust he'll be hit with a trumpet; even the sol crowd demands a quick end for the tortured animal. A *coup de grâce* and the young matador will exit, disgraced.

That night we'll each eat a chicken in San Sebastian and rub the grease into our skin. Years later we'll remember it as the best meal we ever had. Afterward, though, my brother and I will fight. He'll go to Monaco on a forged rail pass and rent a suit. I'll go to Amsterdam but stop in London where I'll watch *The Cook, the Thief, His Wife, and Her Lover* with my uncle. On the train to the ferry terminal in Hull I'll meet three travelers who are about my age. The guy and one of the girls are a couple—a status he'll declare lest I fail to notice their incessant groping. The other girl will be on her way to visit her boyfriend—she'll tell me—in Hull.

Her eyes will stay fixed on mine as she pronounces this detail. In Hull. Oh. She means the prison.

"What for?" I'll ask because I know she wants me to. "For murder." She'll look down. She thinks that's the most interesting thing about her. I'll probably say that it's nice of her to visit him. Or something like that. She'll look up. "Maybe," she'll say, and smile. "Where're you from?" She'll nod and watch my mouth when I speak. When I try to explain the bullfight, she'll put her hand on mine—hold that thought—and excuse herself to the ladies' room. I'll watch her balance her way down the aisle and glance back at me as the train slides forward into the black night.

Christopher Simmons is a Canadian-born, San Francisco-based designer, writer, design advocate, and educator. As principal/creative director of the San Francisco design office, MINE™, he designs and directs brand and communication design projects for clients ranging from Facebook and Microsoft to the Edible Schoolyard Project and Obama for America.

Christopher is an adjunct professor of design at the California College of the Arts (CCA), where he teaches courses in design process, identity design, professional practice and sits on the senior thesis committee.

From 2004 to 2006 he served as president of the San Francisco chapter of AIGA and founded San Francisco Design Week—prompting then mayor Gavin Newsom to issue an official proclamation declaring San Francisco to be a city where "Design Makes a Difference." He is the author of four books and in 2013 was named one of "the 50 most influential designers working today."

The best $10 I ever spent

by Jessica Hische

I was living in Brooklyn and I just bought a brand new fancy camera (a Panasonic Lumix GF1).

I should probably invest in a new camera annually, if only because of the awesome aftermath that accompanies all technology purchases—a feverish excitement to find new and interesting ways to use that technology. If I hadn't been looking for an adventure to document, I don't think I would have found myself in the basement of a fancy ping-pong club in Manhattan in January 2010.

826 NYC, the New York branch of an organization that began in San Francisco (my current home), was throwing a fundraiser—a celebrity ping-pong tournament. The main event featured famous folks (many a few years past their celebrity primes) competing against one another to raise money to help fund 826's writing programs. Mike Meyers was in attendance, as was David Schwimmer, Catherine Keener and writer Sarah Vowell. Dave Eggers, the organization's founder, was also there, the night's silent ringmaster. A couple of years later, he and I would meet in person and I would design the cover to his book *A Hologram for the King*, but at the time I was just another intimidated fan.

It wasn't just celebrities playing—my friend Jeff, who had invited me to the event, found himself competing against another attendee while I tested the 720p video feature of my camera. I must have taken hundreds of blurry pictures that night of '90s celebrity heroes playing ping-pong in short shorts, but the night really got interesting when two smaller fundraising efforts were announced: for fifty dollars, Mike Meyers would record your voicemail message as any of his recognizable movie personas, and for ten dollars you could pay Catherine Keener to slap you in the face.

Photo: Kari Orvik

I immediately ran for the Catherine Keener line.

I noticed quickly that I was the lone lady in a line full of men, which delighted the MC and apparently also Catherine. One by one, each person handed over their ten dollar bill and received a hard slap in the face. When I reached the front of the line, Catherine was delighted that a girl wanted to participate and suggested that I slap her back after she slapped me (at no extra cost!). I had never slapped someone in my life and could barely control my giggling nervousness at the whole prospect.

Shaking out my nervousness, I braced myself for impact and then *crack*, she slapped me in the face! As loud as the sound of her palm hitting my cheek was, it didn't hurt a bit. We both laughed and I got

"

I pretty much punched her in the face with the palm of my hand.

"

ready to reciprocate—checking to make sure Jeff was filming in the sidelines. I gave him an excited and nervous look, pulled my arm back and prepared for the slap.

I pretty much punched her in the face with the palm of my hand.

The noise on impact wasn't the loud sharp crack of a palm hitting a cheek—it was a dull thud, like a big rock being plunked onto soft ground from a great height. I immediately recoiled in horror and apologized profusely. The crowd let out a giant "ohhhh!" groan but Catherine graciously laughed and rescued me from my embarrassment. She came to my side and proceeded to teach me how to slap, explaining that a limp/loose wrist is key (which is why my first attempt failed miserably). I shook it out, as I started to tear up from my own nervousness. She stepped back and awaited my second attempt.

Crack!

The noise was so loud I jumped back and clasped my hands around my mouth in shock. The whole crowd leapt and cheered and shouted. I laughed maniacally and started apologizing before she gave me a big hug. We laughed it off, she complimented me on my slap, and I felt high for the rest of the night. Best ten dollars I ever spent.

Jessica Hische is a letterer, illustrator, and self-described "avid internetter". After graduating with a degree in Graphic and Interactive Design from Tyler School of Art (Temple University) in 2006, she worked for Headcase Design in Philadelphia before taking a position as Senior Designer at Louise Fili Ltd. While working for Louise, she learned most of her skills as a letterer and spent upwards of 16 hours every day working (9 for Louise, 7+ for freelance clients). After two and a half years, Jessica left to further her freelance career and embark on several fun personal projects. Jessica began Daily Drop Cap, a project in which every day she created a new illustrative letter, working through the alphabet a total of twelve times. At its peak, the site had more than 100,000 visitors per month. It culminated with a thirteenth alphabet, each letter crafted by a guest contributor.

Jessica has become as well known for her side projects as she has for her client work. While she doesn't consider herself a web designer, many of her personal projects are web-centric. She's created several educational micro-sites including Mom This is How Twitter Works, Should I Work for Free? and Don't Fear the Internet (with Russ Maschmeyer), each as entertaining as they are helpful. She coined the term "procrastiworking" to describe her tendency to procrastinate on client work by working on personal projects.

Jessica's clients include Wes Anderson, Tiffany & Co., *The New York Times*, Penguin Books, Target, Leo Burnett, American Express, and *Wired* magazine. She has also released several commercial typefaces which are available in her store. Jessica has been named a *Print* magazine New Visual Artist (20 under 30), one of *Forbes* 30 under 30 in Art and Design, an ADC Young Gun, a Person to Watch by *GD USA*, and one of 25 Emerging Artists by *STEP* magazine. She's been personally profiled in many magazines including *Eye* magazine (UK), *Communication Arts*, *Grafik* magazine (UK), and *Novum* magazine (Germany). She is currently serving on the Type Directors Club Board of Directors and divides her time fairly evenly between San Francisco, Brooklyn, and airports en route to design and illustration conferences.

Elegance and toil

by Erik Spiekermann

Many years ago we rented a house near Barberino Val d'Elsa in Tuscany. In the late afternoons we'd go to the little town to drink espresso, eat ice cream and watch life go by.

The road into town was one of those dusty country roads Italians romantically call *strade bianche* (white streets), and it led past a tractor plowing a field. As we passed, the driver took time to greet us before returning to his labor.

Sitting outside the cafe later that day, a little scooter came buzzing along. An elegant gentleman dismounted and waved a friendly greeting at us. We didn't know who he was and didn't speak enough Italian to find out. The next day the tractor driver in the field greeted us once again, this time he acted as though we were old friends. One hour later the man on the scooter turned up and this time involved us in a chat, which tested our knowledge of Italian to the limit. To my eternal embarrassment, we only realized afterwards that he was the friendly tractor driver. His elegant demeanor, fine clothes and charming manner prevented us from making the connection.

My mother would long recall that in Italy even farmers look as though they shop at Armani every day. The lesson at the time was that physical graft, elegance and style needn't necessarily contradict one another.

Erik Spiekermann is information architect, type designer and author. Two of his typefaces, FF Meta and ITC Officina, are considered to be modern classics. He founded MetaDesign (1979) and FontShop (1988). He is behind the design of well-know brands such as Audi, Bosch, VW, German Railways and Heidelberg Printing, among others; information systems for Berlin Transit and Düsseldorf Airport and for publications like *The Economist*.

Erik is Honorary Professor at the University of the Arts in Bremen and in 2003 received the Gerrit Noordzij Award from the Royal Academy in The Hague. In 2006, he was awarded an honorary doctorship from Pasadena Art Center. He was made an Honorary Royal Designer for Industry by the RSA in Britain in 2007 and Ambassador for the European Year of Creativity and Innovation by the European Union for 2009.

In 2011, he received the German National Design Award for Lifetime Achievement and the TDC Medal. Today he is managing partner and creative director of Edenspiekermann with offices in Berlin, Amsterdam and San Francisco.

What's in a name?

by Allan Chochinov

Well, yeah, I grew up with the name Allan Chochinov and nobody really thinks of Allan with two Ls, and, if they do, it's Allen. And they *certainly* don't know how to spell Chochinov. So it's a chore.

My sister Dena changed her name to Deena when she was a teenager, tired of people calling her *Deh-nah* rather than

Dee-nah. That inspired me, but of course changing my name to Alan wouldn't have helped (I'm actually not so fond of that spelling) and that wasn't really the root of my challenge.

....

So I trudged through: The first days of my grade school years were predictably dreaded, but I got older and naturally began to appreciate uniqueness over simplicity.

....

The truth is that my name actually has a wonderful simplicity—in its nickname: Choch. Indeed, *all* of the Chochinovs in Winnipeg, where I grew up and where the name is not such an anomaly (you might want to stop by Chochinov Park when you're next in town), are nicknamed Choch. It's fun and short and actually easy to spell, too. I remember being at a family reunion—imagine one hundred Chochinovs in a cousin's backyard—and someone yelled out "Choch!" Everyone turned. It was funny. And kind of embarrassing. And funny.

All grown up, the real challenge with having a last name like mine is in the spelling—with businesses, with people on the phone, with travel agents (remember them?), with, well, anyone who needs to take my name over the phone. And so my strategies got scientific.

For years I would mimic what my parents (Ethel and Earl) did, and still do: I'd split Chochinov into three neat triplets. "My last name? Sure. It's c-h-o . . . c-h-i . . . n-o-v." The trouble with this one is that after you've said the c-h-o part, right when you begin the c-h-"Wait! One sec: Is it 'c-h-o', or 'c-h-i'?" Because the first parts are so similar, this method of spelling out raised a new kind of confusion.

So around the age of twenty I got clever: I figured I'd group up the letters in a different way: "My last name? Sure. It's c-h-o-c-h . . . i-n . . . o-v." Well, it turns out that the five-letter, near-palindromic "c-h-o-c-h" is often too much for the listener to parse in one shot. And even when it *does* work, the C can be mistaken for a T, the H sounds like an 8 and then there's the killer letter at end, V. Which sounds like a B. Or a Z. So now, I'm like, "o-v, as in Victor"—which sounds old and out of style, except that my wife's name is Victoria, (which, if used, would be gender confusing), so I stick with Victor. But I kind of feel like a dork using Victor, though it is the official NATO military alphabet name for the letter. I can't imagine that you feel my pain, exactly, but remember that I need to deal with this *every day of my life*.

So now I've got a daughter, and we named her Bronwyn (okay, yes, that's a whole lotta name, Bronwyn Chochinov), and it will soon be time for her to start spelling her name on the phone to people. (We gave her the middle name Elvis, by the way, to basically cut her some slack.) She recently overheard me spelling out my name on the phone, and when I hung up she asked me why I did the c-h-o-c-h instead of the c-h-o, and I tried to explain it and then figured I'd just write it out. So this story is for her, really.

In any event, to cut to the chase, I recently was honored to write a piece for Steven Heller's book *Design Disasters*.

I wrote something on the notion of failure in which I iterated the same paragraph—about failure—several times until I ended up back where I began (the first paragraph version).

I was happy with it, and soon after, Victoria and I ran into Steve in the neighborhood, and he was really excited that the book was coming out shortly and said that he'd get me a copy.

We joked with Steve that with a book named *Design Disasters*, he would be forgiven any and all errors—from typographic to grammar— and that for this one, at least, he'd be completely off the hook; nothing to worry about.

A few weeks passed, and in my mailbox arrived a brand new, hot-off-the-press copy of *Design Disasters*. My piece was the first in the collection (so proud) and after thumbing through the rest of the book I turned to the back cover to read the lineup of contributors.

Then I read my name in the list: Allan Chocinov.

I smiled. If you're going to put up with your name being misspelled, you have to be pretty jazzed that it's misspelled on the back cover of a book called *Design Disasters*. Thank you, Steve! I may not have gotten the credit, but I got the story.

....

Allan Chochinov is a partner of Core77, a New York–based design network serving a global community of designers and design enthusiasts, and Chair of the new MFA in Products of Design graduate program at the School of Visual Arts in New York City. Prior, his work in product design focused on the medical, surgical, and diagnostic fields, as well as on consumer products and workplace systems. He has been named on numerous design and utility patents and serves on the boards of the AIGA, Designers Accord, the Camraderie, Design Ignites Change, and DesigNYC. He has taught at the graduate and undergraduate level since 1995.

Fortune cookies

by Pamela Williams

When I was in college, I worked in a Chinese restaurant. I'd never have applied to work there if it hadn't been for my best friend, Ann, who also wanted to work there and insisted it would be fun.

Neither of us looked the part, me with blonde hair and Ann with her smiling Irish eyes, titian hair and freckles. Our uniforms were red silk kimonos, the same color as the cherries that garnished the drinks we served, black pants, and serviceable black shoes. We went to work with our hair rolled up into a bun, finished with two chopsticks that made Xs. I wish had a photo of the two of us from back then, but when you're young you don't realize then that these times will someday be the good old days.

The owner loved us, but the manager of the restaurant, not so much. No matter how much extra work we did (she called it side work) or how many compliments customers gave us, we could never find our way into Cranky Manager's good graces. She thought we didn't take our work seriously. (We did, we had to: we lived off our tips. Our monthly paychecks, combined, couldn't cover the electric bill.)

As hard as we worked, we had great times. After our evening shift, we'd leave the restaurant, each carrying two quart-size paper soup containers. One would be stuffed with tips and the other, a to-go beverage. Once we'd finally get to our home near the beach, we'd dump out our tips on the living room floor. One of us would sort, count and roll the change, the other would stack the ones and fives. And we'd both sip our Tonga Punches through straws (or whatever drink our favorite bartender had concocted for us that night), while we told stories of customers and laughed. We never failed to make our rent, and if any of our friends ever needed change, they knew who to ask.

None of the cooks spoke English, but we knew they liked us. At least, they sure smiled a lot. Cranky Manager wasn't anymore Chinese than Ann or I, but she thought we had way too much fun.

One time she checked our workstations during a shift and discovered the tiki cocktails we'd hide for ourselves every night.

Our tikis were tucked between the replica mango platters, the cast-iron braziers and the Sterno we used to fire up the Pu Pu platters. (We later tucked the drinks behind the stack of large serving trays we knew she couldn't lift.) To curry favor with Cranky Manager, one day we decided to memorize every dish on the menu.

We thought it would astound her, and for us, it was an amusing diversion between studying and working.

One night, with our "homework" complete, we arrived extra early to do our side work. We filled dishes with mustard and duck sauces, cleaned and refilled the soy sauce bottles, and stocked our stations with chopsticks. We went into the kitchen just before dinner service and stood side by side in front of the cook station, the place where you stand when you are ready to place an order.

We held hands, took a deep breath, and in perfect unison said aloud every item on the menu from soups to apps to entrees and desserts: Luck Drop Soup, Egg Drop Soup, Pu Pu Platter, Beef Teriyaki on Skewer, BBQ Spare Ribs, Hong Shei Gai, Moo Goo Gai Pan, Sesame Chicken, Kong Po Chicken, Shrimp in Lobster Sauce, Orange Beef, Dragon Palace Special Fried Rice, Pistachio Ice Cream, Slice Fresh Pineapple, Bowl of Fresh Fruit, Lychee Fruit with Cherry—all seventy-nine items!

The recitation took us maybe three minutes, tops. We high-fived. The kitchen staff broke into laughter. I remember hearing a smattering of applause. The owner nodded three times, meaning he liked it. Even Cranky Manager cracked a small smile. We hightailed it out of the kitchen to finish setting our tables. A few minutes later, we heard the chef's bell ring. Then again. And again. Why were we being summoned to the kitchen?

We ran down the two flights of stairs and pushed through the swinging kitchen door. Whoa! The kitchen smelled great, and the service counters were piled with freshly cooked foods: Pu Pu Platter, Hong She Gai, Moo Goo Gai Pan, Shrimp and Lobster sauce, Luck Drop Soup, Spare Ribs, Shrimp in Lobster Sauce ...

Wow!

Almost everything on the menu!

Wait, no.

The kitchen staff had made every single item on the menu.

And that is the story of the first time I got fired.

Pamela Williams is the creative director at Williams and House, which she cofounded years after tending bar, hostessing and waitressing her way through college. Now she works at an organic farm on Fridays and gets paid in French Breakfast radishes and heirloom tomatoes.

Formsache

by Stefan Bucher

A few years ago I needed to travel back home to Germany. A week before I was set to fly out I noticed that my passport had expired, so I made my way to the German consulate on Wilshire Boulevard here in Los Angeles to apply for an emergency replacement.

After all this time living in California it's always a bit of a head-trip for me to be among a lot of German speakers again, particularly at an early hour when I should still be fast asleep. It feels like a strange but orderly dream. I'd been to this office a few times over the years. It looks as if a German post office had been teleported whole into the eleventh-floor corner suite of an office building. Once you climb above a certain elevation, you no longer expect to see service counters or pens on chains—or a security gate manned by a burly guard—but there they were.

Photo: Jill Greenberg

After a short wait, a consular officer called my name handed me the appropriate form. I filled it out, handed it back to him and was told to return for my passport the next day. No fuss, no muss.

As ordered, I came back the next morning, bleary-eyed as on the day before—up the elevator, past the guard, through the security gate, and into the waiting area. When my turn came, I stepped up to the counter and took my seat before the officer—not the same one, I noticed, who had seen me the previous day. I told him my name and that I was here to pick up my emergency passport. "You were here yesterday to hand in your form?" Yes. "You filled out the form yourself?"

What now? Had I filled it out myself? I wondered what this meant. Was this the same kind of question as "Did you pack your own suitcase?" Was I in trouble somehow?

"Yes, I filled out the form myself," I said. Gulp. Slight darting of the eyes to check for possible escape routes.

"One moment." The officer turned around to the people working at the desks in the back. "It's him."

It's him?! I'm him?! Who? What?

I could see a few of the other officers peeking out from behind their monitors to look at me with curiosity.

What the hell was going on? When you're dealing with government agents, you learn not to ask questions, but this was just too odd.

"Excuse me, sir. What just happened here?" I asked.

"Oh, not to worry. We just had never seen a form filled out so neatly, and the others wanted to see who you were."

And there you have it. You know you've crossed into a strange, new territory of obsessive achievement when the German government compliments you on the neatness of your forms. Feel free to fear me.

Stefan G. Bucher is the man behind 344lovesyou.com and the popular online drawing and story-telling experiment dailymonster.com. He is the author of the books *100 Days of Monsters*, *All Access*, *The Graphic Eye*, *You Deserve a Medal—Honors on the Path to True Love*, *344 Questions—The Creative Person's Do-It-Yourself Guide to Insight, Survival, and Artistic Fulfillment*, and *The Yeti Story*, which he wrote and illustrated exclusively for Saks Fifth Avenue. He has created designs for David Hockney, Judd Apatow, and *The New York Times*. D&AD honored him with a Yellow Pencil for book design, and the Art Directors Club of New York declared him a Young Gun back in 2004. He designed the titles for the motion pictures *The Fall*, *Immortals*, and *Mirror, Mirror* by director Tarsem, and his time-lapse drawings appear on the Emmy-award winning TV show The Electric Company on PBS.

Celebrate Columbus

by James Victore

I told the story about the making of my first poster, Celebrate Columbus (1992), in my book, *Victore or, Who Died and Made You Boss?* (You *have* read my book, right?)

"Celebrate Columbus" came from my own desires and frustrations as a designer to use my abilities to comment on the news, society and culture. I had no idea what I was getting into. I just wanted to make a statement with a poster. Projects like Kickstarter were not around at the time (hell, the internet was not around at the time), and certainly there was no client I could find to fund my opinion. Nevertheless I pressed on and used what little money I had—my rent money—to print and wheat paste 1,500 posters around NYC. Thus began an obsession with posters and a bad business plan.

The one story I have never told about this period of my life was the eviction notices. Every few months, the doorbell would ring and waiting downstairs was a man in a suit. "You are served," was his only line.

I wish I had saved these papers. I would have had them beautifully photographed and put into my book. These legal notices were proof of my conviction—the cost of my freedom—the price I had to pay to make posters. My girlfriend at the time was really not happy with me and left. She was the price, too.

....

James Victore is an author, designer, filmmaker, artist and firestarter who teaches creatives how to illuminate their individual gifts in order to achieve personal greatness. Described as "part Darth Vader, part Yoda," James is widely known for his timely wisdom and impassioned views about design and its place in the world. He reaches thousands online with his weekly Q+A video series and leads game-changing workshops and seminars that help creative types of all spheres live and work successfully. At the helm of his independently run design studio, James continually strives to make work that is sexy, strong and memorable; work that tows the line between the sacred and the profane.

James' work has been exhibited by the Museum of Modern Art in New York and is represented in the permanent collections of museums worldwide. His clients include Bobbi Brown Cosmetics, Moet & Chandon, Aveda, *TIME Magazine*, Yohji Yamamoto, *Esquire Magazine* and *The New York Times*. Awards include an Emmy for television animation, and Gold and Silver Medals from the New York Art Director's Club. His work was recently published in a monograph titled *Victore or, Who Died and Made You Boss?* Victore teaches at the School of Visual Arts in NYC. He lives, loves and works in Brooklyn.

The light

by Alexander Isley

I once ran a searchlight from a car dealership parking lot. My job was to draw in customers like moths to a really big (800 million candlepower) flame.

This was really my friend's job, but one night he hadn't been able to make it and asked me to fill in. I'm glad I did.

It all seemed simple enough: Show up to the lot, sit next to a huge light, shine it up into the sky for four hours, and get paid for the effort. That was all there was to it, and to be honest the whole thing seemed kind of easy (and kind of silly) to me. What was the point? There was no special sale or radio promotion, no "look for the light" advertising, or any other real reason for the light to be there or for people to care.

Nevertheless, it promised to require little effort and I'd make some cash while sitting around. It was a perfect job for a lazy high school student with no experience or qualifications. In other words, the position dovetailed seamlessly with my skill set.

I brought a folding chair along with a book to help pass the time over to the Toyota dealership on highway 15-501 near Chapel Hill, North Carolina, ready for inaction. There I met the owner of the searchlight rental company (cleverly named Searchlight Rental) who showed me the how to operate the machinery.

The searchlight was huge, a 60-inch diameter olive drab WWII vintage army surplus unit, mounted along with a generator on a trailer. It was similar to the model that came with my childhood G.I. Joe Jeep Combat Set. Only this version was larger, not made of plastic, and it didn't have a light bulb.

Instead, a bright white flame was produced by a carbon arc lamp burner mounted in front of an enormous coated mirror that beamed the light up and out. The light was generated by igniting 18-inch carbon rods that burned down as they were slowly fed into the reflector mechanism by an array of small gears.

Every 90 minutes or so I would have to open a small hatch, climb into the unit, and replace the rods as they burned down. If I neglected to do this and one burned through to the end, the whole trailer would explode. Or so the boss informed me.

And with that he shook my hand, wished me good luck, and left for the night.

I realized I was not going to be able to just sit there and relax at all, and I put the book away. At dusk I started the generator, fired up the light, and pointed it up into the night. It was a little cloudy so the beam was well defined. I was excited.

And it worked. People began to show up. Over the next few hours an ongoing stream people drove into the lot to discover the source of the light and pepper me with questions, none of which I was equipped to address.

They came from all over. Many had driven for up to 45 minutes "just to see what's going on." Veterans walked up to me, sharing experiences from the war. Parents made pilgrimages with their kids. High school students dropped by to hang out.

This was more than just a searchlight. It was Friday night entertainment, and I was the adventitious MC, fielding technical questions (and responding insufficiently) while keeping a nervous eye on flaming carbon sticks as they slowly ground down toward cataclysm.

None of these people had come to the parking lot with the idea of buying a Toyota, but that didn't stop the sales guys who hovered at a distance and took turns picking off their marks as they got tired of the light and me. I was impressed with the (and there is no other word for it, as far as I'm concerned) fearlessness they showed in approaching complete strangers and launching right into a friendly pitch. I wish I could do that.

At the end of the night I shut down the generator (no meltdowns or explosions, thankfully) and climbed inside the glass enclosure to wipe down the carbon residue with Windex and paper towels.

And that was it. I went to the dealership manager for payment. That was the only disappointing part of the night. He seemed a bit condescending and smirked as he wrote out the check to Searchlight Rental, and I remember feeling defensive and suddenly loyal to my new, one-time employer as I realized that it was actually quite a perfect name for the company—there was no mistaking what they did and it was an easy name to remember.

So no need to be jerky, Mr. Manager. We all gotta work, and while I didn't get to show up in nice khaki slacks with pleats and wear cologne, at least I got to wear a T-shirt to work, be in charge of an awesome piece of military surplus hardware capable of lighting up the night and possibly exploding, and having an excuse to talk to new girls (who were coming up to *me*).

Anyway, that was the first and last time I ran the light, but the things I learned that special night I use every day:

- One must first attract attention in order to be able to convey a message.

- People are inherently curious and will often make great effort to pursue and learn about something that seems mysterious.

- People respond to things that are big, bright, and unusual.

- You learn the most when you have no idea what you are doing.

- Jobs that might seem boring at first often turn out to be quite interesting.

- If something works well it doesn't really matter that it might be old.

- A Sperry anti-aircraft searchlight is an outstanding conversation starter.

- Getting people to show up is half the battle.

- Don't be shy—if you don't engage people you have no hope of making a sale.

- In naming a company or service, it's better to be simple and descriptive rather than clever and confusing.

- If you don't pay close attention to all the details, things will explode.

....

Alexander Isley began his career in the early 1980s as the senior designer at Tibor Kalman's influential M&Co. He then served as the art director of the funny and fearless *Spy magazine*. In 1988 he founded Alexander Isley Inc. in New York City.

Alex has been a lecturer and critic in the graduate program of the Yale School of Art and has served as an instructor at the Cooper Union and the School of Visual Arts, teaching courses in design and typography.

He is past president of AIGA New York and is a recipient of the 2013 AIGA Fellow award. Alex was elected a member of AGI and was an inaugural member of "The I.D. 40," *I.D. Magazine's* survey of the country's leading design innovators. Alex was recently named as one of the most influential designers of the past 50 years by readers of *GDUSA magazine*.

His work is in the collections of the Museum of Modern Art, the Smithsonian Institution, and the Library of Congress.

One thing always leads to another

by Ji Lee

The following story shows how a small project I experimented with while I was at school lead me to meet one of the most important people in the history of mankind and then to find my dream job.

Many years ago, in a galaxy far, far away, I studied graphic design at Parsons New School for Design. While I was in my third year, the school introduced its first computer lab. This was a very historic and exciting event. I learned the first design programs such as Quark Xpress, Photoshop, Illustrator and a crude 3-D program called Adobe Dimensions (which doesn't exist anymore). One of the tools that I was playing with was called "revolve," which allowed you to draw a two-dimensional shape and revolve it around an axis to form a 3-D object. I thought this was a really fun thing to do. In one of my fun experiments, I decided to revolve the letters of the alphabet. It was amazing to see how each letter when revolved, formed a beautiful and unique 3-D shape. When I rotated the twenty-six letters of the alphabet, I realized I had created a new 3-D font by accident. I wanted to give it a cool name, so I took a font with a futuristic and spacey name Univers and I called it Univers Revolved.

After my graduation, I worked in several design firms. Although the work was busy and I was learning a lot, I really wanted to work in advertising because I was interested in ideas and scale. So I quit my job at a corporate design firm, and I started to freelance while I was trying to get my foot into advertising. But I didn't really know how I could do this, since I didn't know anyone in advertising. I was freelancing at a well-regarded design studio called Design/Writing/ Research founded by Abbott Miller. At the time, Abbott was publishing a book called *Dimensional Typography*, which featured several computer-generated 3D fonts. He saw my Univers Revolved font in my portfolio; he liked it and included it in his book. After the book was published, *The New York Times* was publishing a special Sunday magazine dedicated to technology. One of the editors saw the *Dimensional Typography* book, liked my font and contacted me. The font ended up published in *The New York Times*. At the same time, Saatchi & Saatchi, one of the most famous advertising agencies in the world, was organizing its first Innovation in Communication Award. They invited several influential and famous artists, scientists and authors as judges. One of the judges for the award was Laurie Anderson, a musician and a poet. Laurie saw my 3-D font in *The New York Times* magazine and told Saatchi people to contact me to enter the award. One day I got an email from Saatchi inviting me to enter the award with my Univers Revolved font. I did and it became one of the ten finalists. Saatchi & Saatchi organized a dinner with all finalists and judges at a fancy midtown restaurant in New York. I was so excited. As a young designer who dreamed of working in advertising, this was beyond my dream come true. At the dinner, I was seated at a round table of about ten people. Right next to me, there was a gentleman in his 70s. He had white hair; he was dressed in a power suit; he had an expensive watch on his wrist and a huge presence. For some reason, I was certain he was one of the Saatchi brothers I had read about in newspapers and magazines. To be polite, I struck a conversation and here's exactly how it went.

Me: Hi, I'm Ji Lee. Nice to meet you.
He: Hello. Nice to meet you.
Me: So, do you work at Saatchi?
He: No.
Me: What do you do?
He: I'm an astronaut.
Me: Wow. [Pause] When was the last time you were in space?
He: 1969.
Me: (silence)

I tried to figure out what exactly happened in 1969. It took me about three seconds to realize he was one of the first three men to land on the Moon. He was *the* Buzz Aldrin.

"

I asked him if he believed in UFOs. He quickly said, 'No,' and followed with: 'But I have seen things I can't really explain.' And I was thinking: *That sounds just like UFOs.*

"

I felt immediately humbled and honored, and my heart was racing. Eventually I calmed myself down, and Buzz and I ended up having some great conversations. One of the most memorable parts of our conversation that night was when I asked him if he believed in UFOs.

He quickly said, "No," and followed with: "But I have seen things I can't really explain." And I was thinking: *That sounds just like UFOs.*

In the end, I didn't win the Saatchi's Award, but I did end up meeting Bob Isherwood, who was then Saatchi's worldwide creative officer. Bob liked my work and offered me a job as an art director at Saatchi.

I think about how a fun school project led me from one person to another over the years, until I got to one of the first men on the moon at a dinner table, and later, to my dream job. It's funny how the universe has its way of granting your wish. And it made me realize that personal projects that I have passion for—that I have fun with—always lead to amazing people and life-changing opportunities. Experiences like this have made me into an evangelist who spreads the message about the transformative power of personal projects.

Ah, and one more amazing story resulted from this extraordinary chain of events. I ended up meeting Laurie Anderson, who discovered my 3-D font in *The New York Times Magazine*. To thank her, I invited her and her boyfriend, Lou Reed, and their dog, Lola, to my apartment for a dinner. But this is a story to be told in the next book.)

Born in Seoul, Korea, and raised in São Paulo, Brazil, Ji Lee moved to New York to study graphic design. Ji has been working in the fields of design, advertising, technology and art.

Ji works as a creative strategist at Facebook. His past jobs include Google, Droga 5 and Saatchi & Saatchi. In addition to his professional work, Ji is also dedicated to his personal projects. Some of his well-known projects include the Bubble Project, Word as Image and Wordless Web.

In 2011, Ji was listed as one of the 50 most influential designers in the United States by *Fast Company* magazine. Ji Lee is the author of three books: *Word as Image, Talk Back: The Bubble Project,* and *Univers Revolved: A 3-D Alphabet.* Ji's work has appeared in *ABC World News, Wired, Fast Company,* and *Oprah.* Ji is a frequent contributor for the *New York Times.*

Balloon animals

by Brian Singer

Another friend was getting married. This is what happens after college. First one, then another, until the years blend into a blur of suits, ceremonies and, of course, bachelor parties.

It was a Friday afternoon, and I was meeting up with two friends, Bob and Donovan, to make the drive up to Lake Tahoe for yet another of these bachelor parties. We met at Bob's work, parked our cars and piled into his SUV. Knowing how bad traffic can be at that time, we decided to grab a bite to eat before the long drive.

There's a place near Bob's work called McCarthy Ranch, which is essentially a collection of stores and chain restaurants. This is where we went, and don't ask me how or why, but we found ourselves at Applebee's. Don't judge me.

The place was packed, and we found a high table in the bar area. Midway through the meal, a girl came up to us. A balloon girl. You've seen them before; they walk around restaurants and offer to make balloon animals or hats for little kids. The parents awkwardly accept, and then try to figure out how much to pay for the balloon. What's the going rate for an obnoxious hat, after all?

I'd guess she was twenty or so, not unattractive. She approached us and said, "Hey guys, would you like a balloon animal?"

Donovan looked at her, and then looked around the restaurant at all the tables and other families before settling back on her.

Perplexed, he asked, "Out of all the familes in this restaurant, what makes you think *we* would want a balloon animal?"

She looked taken aback and a bit uncomfortable. Now, shyly, she said, "Well, I can make some pretty cool stuff, and I just thought you guys might like the stuff I can make."

I felt bad for her. She's just trying to make a living but had clearly picked the wrong table to solicit. But really, what are three men going to do with a balloon animal?

Donovan continued, "Okay, what cool stuff can you make?"

She looked around, and then leaned in and quietly whispered into my ear, "I can make two monkeys butt-fucking."

I sat there in silence, staring across the restaurant, contemplating the meaning of life. This girl was good. She pegged us from the moment we sat down, and we walked right into it.

A moment passed in silence and finally Bob impatiently asked, "Well, what can she make?"

I turned to Donovan, and then Bob, and calmly stated, "We're getting a balloon animal."

....

Brian Singer considered duplicating someone else's bio here and seeing if any noticed but was advised against it. How about this instead, if you send him a self-addressed stamped envelope, he promises to send you some goodies. His address is 3907 23rd Street, San Francisco, CA, 94114. While you're at it, let him know how you feel about writing in the third-person. He finds it dreadfully awkard.

Don't worry, he's not dumb, he's just fucking lazy

by Armin Vit

After being invited to contribute to this book, I first considered writing about the time a raccoon came into our kitchen through the pet door and the weeklong battle that ensued to capture him (or her) as we saw him (or her) as a threat to our cats, since he (or she)—let's just call it it—was after their kibble.

Long story short, since this is not the story I want to tell in detail: a hipster transplant to Austin, Texas, from Brooklyn, New York, set up a trail of marshmallows leading up to two traps that captured not just "it," but one other raccoon and two possums in the course of two weeks. That was almost three years ago. About six months ago, though, we saw a raccoon walk across our backyard in broad daylight. We couldn't help but wonder if it was "it" (or him or her) and how many more were out there. I've since eaten all the marshmallows, so our chances of catching "it" are slim.

The story I do want to tell relates to graphic design, and it's about how I came to be a graphic designer. Not because I'm the most celebrated figure in the field or because my upbringing in it is worthy of chronicling, but because it always surprises people who assume I had graphic design as a higher calling. The reason I became a designer is pretty simple: I had to go to college and study something, but I had absolutely zero ambitions of being anything in particular. I chose graphic design, because I figured it wouldn't demand too many written tests or learning *stuff*. This was a main concern of mine because in high school I sucked as a student.

In Mexico City—where I was born, raised and schooled until I graduated college—grades are given on a scale from 0 to 10, instead of the American A, B, C, D and F system or the 0 to 4 GPA system. To move up from grade to grade, students must achieve an average grade across all courses of 6.0; 5.9 is a fail. Junior high wasn't too bad. If memory serves me correctly, I passed each of the three years with an 8.0 or so average. But high school was a mess. Each year, I barely passed with a 6-point-something average. They handed out grade cards every three or four months. In many courses I would manage to score a paltry 4, eventually getting an 8 to average a 6. Each time my mom had to be called into the principal's office to be told that I had to get it together or that they would hold me back a year. My senior high school year, after one of those meetings, my best friend at the time pulled my mom aside and said, "Don't worry. He's not dumb. He's just fucking lazy."

He was right. For sure on the latter assessment of my laziness but the former would take years to prove and me to realize. I had no interest in school. I hated biology, chemistry, math, history, civics and pretty much everything else, including the four or five courses taught in Hebrew, since I attended a private Jewish school. (I know!)

(And, yes, *ani medaver kzat hibrit.*) The only two courses I excelled at were English (which is why me write so pretty) and etymology, where I found that I had an innate knack to understand where words came from and how they were formed. Other than that, my main concerns in high school—1992 to 1995—were playing video games on the Sega Genesis (I was a master at all things Electronic Arts), listening to heavy metal (Metallica's *Black Album* dropped at the time), and playing basketball and watching it on television (Go, Bulls!). Studying for an exam totally got in the way of those three things, so I studied enough to get a 6.0. No more, usually less. Of my high school performance the only thing that indicated I should go into graphic design was that I could faithfully redraw the logos of Metallica, Iron Maiden, and Van Halen on the notebooks inside which I was supposed to be taking class notes. But there was another reason that I ended up studying graphic design: my dad.

A mathematician by trade, with a Ph.D. in some complicated combination of math, physics and theories of lines (as in lines of people), my dad inherited my grandfather's business—VitaDrog, a buyer and seller of the core ingredients of pharmaceutical products—when my grandfather passed away. A businessman by day, my dad always had an interest in computing and computers and as far as I remember there was always a computer in my house where I played everything from *Where in the World Is Carmen Sandiego?* to *Leisure Suit Larry.* In the early 1990s my dad bought one of the first Macs, intrigued by the premise of a graphic interface and a mouse. He loved it. He purchased Adobe Illustrator 88—yes, that's before the 1.0 version and way before CS versions or this thing called Creative Cloud—and started playing with it, making layouts of whoknowswhat and printing them out. Somehow he ended up interested in graphic design and subscribed to magazines and bought books. Then, just like that, he went back to college to study it. The rational thing would have probably been to stop running his business, but there were still mortgages and my expensive high school tuition to be paid so he did both things. He went to class early in the morning, then went to work, then took an evening class, then came home to have dinner with us, then he did his homework.

He did posters, book covers, logos and other stuff by hand and on his Mac. Books with the work of things called Pentagram and of people named Milton Glaser and Paul Rand invaded his personal desk, which used to only hold a calculator, a stapler and a letter opener before all this. I watched with interest, not because of the artifacts he created or the books he read but in amazement that you could go to college and muck around with shit and call it a career. So when I finally graduated with a 6.3 grade average my senior year and had to choose a career path, I went into graphic design because, above all, it looked like the path of least resistance.

One thing you should know about graphic design in Mexico in the 1990s is that it was considered an easy thing to do, and the path to becoming a professional graphic designer was also easy, fun even.

As horrible as this sounds (and this is not a prejudice I came up with but an acknowledged situation): A lot of upper-class girls went into graphic design while their fiancés went to business management school so that they could work at their daddy's business and make tons of money and then marry each other. Graphic design was known as an MMC: Mientras Me Caso ("While I Marry" or "WIM" in English). I had no girlfriend at the time, no intention of going into my dad's business, and I was one of two boys in a class of twenty-two; all girls with varying degrees of engagement status and levels of little to nonexistent interest in graphic design. Hardly the environment I needed to gain interest in the field.

This was a four-year graphic design course. No liberal arts, no majors or minors, just graphic design all the time. Being 1995, and with Mexico the slow adopter of technology that it is, my education in graphic design was pretty old school: logos were traced by hand, layouts were completed with pasted galleys and mechanicals were done with paper overlays with registration marks that I had to make myself.

The first two years kind of sucked. For one, there was an art history class that required testing and memorizing, and then there were assignments like carving a potato to make a stamp, inking it and making stupid patterns. Most girls in my class used most assignments to create mementos for their fiancés. *Hurl.* I even managed to flunk "natural drawing" class because I couldn't draw things like a bottle of Coca-Cola or a piece of fruit—I had to retake the class as a summer intensive and missed out on a trip to Vancouver with my parents.

By the third year, things got more interesting; we were doing logos, stationery, packaging, iconography and editorial layouts. I was getting into it. Having a Mac at home and a fully stocked library, thanks to my dad's interest, gave me an edge. I knew who David Carson was and that *Emigre* was a magazine and a seller of digital fonts. As my interest in graphic design grew, my patience for the attitude and lack of interest of my fellow lady classmates shrank.

During your typical class "crits" (critiques), with work hanging on the wall, most of the students would either say nothing or, if they did, it was to say how pretty the work was. Even the teachers were quite the wusses and offered little to no criticism, as they knew their words fell on deaf ears, or they simply didn't want to haggle with a whiny girl about how she deserved a ten and not a nine.

So I started to be a ravaging critic. Mainly because I enjoyed antagonizing the other students but also because I was actually enjoying the process of formulating thoughts about why something worked or didn't work. I was never mean, but I was always honest and the lack of investment in their work was shooting-fish-in-a-barrel easy. I was labeled the "class jerk." Who would have thought that one day I would be a professional "jerk," critiquing logos and identity work, literally, for a living on our blog Brand New? But I digress, this story is not about what I do now but how I ended up here.

The truth might actually be that graphic design was indeed a higher calling for me. Perhaps it was just one shelf too high for my lazy ass to want to reach. But sometime during that third year of college I discovered that graphic design was something I was good at, that I understood and was willing—or, more importantly, happily willing—to spend as many hours as needed to get it done right. Even when it meant foregoing hours of playing video games or watching the Bulls take a sixth NBA title. Luckily I could still crank the Metallica and get my homework done. I wasn't "fucking lazy" anymore. Still a little dumb, but not lazy. Well, a little lazy: I guess I could have gone to the grocery store to get some more marshmallows to catch that elusive raccoon.

The little dog in the little red sweater

by Jennifer Sterling

My first office.

Or rather what I felt was my first real office space after leaving a space within an ad agency located on Maiden Lane in San Francisco—I leased a new loft space in the SOMA district. Signing at the time what I thought were mountains of legalese, I was now the proud lessee of a two-story loft, albeit carpeted and wall-to-wall carpet to boot—something I've yet to see again in a brand-new loft space.

First on the agenda is to remedy this.

I was fortunate that my fiancé at the time (Marko) was handy in this area. He quite good-naturedly set upon ripping out the carpet and replacing it with hardwood floors. He began this with the help of my son (Jonathan, then thirteen) and Jonathan's perpetual shadow, his best friend, Tony.

Day 1: Some sort of bitter storm in San Francisco (rare now), I'm carrying a mountain of things up to my new loft. Four flights up the back staircase I'm perspiring and exhausted when Marko greats me at the door with, "You're not going to be happy." This is in response to my question, "Where's Jonathan?" After a few moments of explanation, I discover the boys were on the balcony and one of them (not Jonathan) spit over the ledge onto a "little dog in a little red sweater."

Marko goes downstairs to apologize to the owner of the dog, only to discover that he is the lawyer who was head of the co-op and whose mountains of legalese I had just signed—most importantly, a lengthy clause having to do with "the behavior of tenants and subsequent eviction." This apology gets nowhere as the lawyer does not wish to speak to Marko.

I find Jonathan locked in the bathroom.

He opens the door after hearing my wrath.

After several minutes of me saying things like, "Do you think this is a joke? My getting kicked out after putting $40,000 into a new studio—after one day," and his, *sob ... sob ... sob ...* we head down the back stairwell for him to make amends.

Tony lurks behind as we encounter the "little dog in the little red sweater."

"Is that the dog?" I ask. Jonathan sobs and nods.

I knock on the door only to be greeted by a beautiful, icy, Nordic woman named Pamela.

I introduce myself and profess my weird family genealogy in the following manner: "Hello, my name is Jennifer Sterling and I've just taken the loft upstairs. Apparently there was an incident earlier today.

One of the boys (not mine) apparently spit over the balcony and, um... it landed on... um... your dog. I don't know how this happened. We come from a long line of nonspitters."

Pamela folds her arms and questions whether this will be a recurring incident. I assure her it will not.

During this encounter I see a man in the background of her loft installing something on the ceiling and a man (whom I can only assume to be the "angry" lawyer) brushes by me—without a nod—despite my repeated apology, introduction, and claims of nonspitting lineage.

I'm at this point trying to do the correct thing by suggesting how Jonathan (who did not do this) might make amends by working for them for the next few hours before we leave for the day, as well as returning the following day to do some additional chores.

At this time another new neighbor appears (great) the architect, Mitchell, who lives in the loft across from mine.

"

One of the boys (not mine) apparently spit over the balcony and um... it landed on... um... your dog. I don't know how this happened. We come from a long line of nonspitters.

"

I ramble "nonspitting genealogy introduction" and close the deal with Pamela for Jonathan's list of chores. We set a time for me to return to pick him up.

Mitchell and I trudge upstairs with Tony still lurking. I fill Marko in on the events while I make introductions. After a few moments Mitchell asks me if I know what Pamela does.

"No what?"

"She's a dominatrix," he replies.

Marko meanwhile is trying to make out why was in that apartment anyway—as that balcony couldn't possibly be below ours.

"Well, I followed the little dog in the little red sweater ..." I find myself stammering.

I hurry downstairs (Tony following) and rap on Pamela's door. The site of Jonathan vacuuming in the background greets this intuitive and responsible mother who has (inadvertently) left her son in an (apparent) dominatrix's loft.

The only explanation I could come up with is that Pamela must own both lofts. Otherwise why would she let my son make amends in this loft? (A part of my brain scolds the other for being concerned with this line of reasoning—and not her apparent occupation.)

I blurt out my inquiry about dual loft ownership to Pamela only to have it met with, "Oh no I don't own both, but the guys across the hall are so difficult to deal with."

I'm not sure what else she was going to say. I collect my son and inform Pamela that Jonathan will not be returning tomorrow as previously agreed.

As we enter my loft I hear Tony remark to Jonathan, "Dude, I think you were in the wrong loft."

After much back and forth between them I hear Jonathan lament to Tony, "What are the chances of two stupid little dogs in two stupid little red sweaters in the same building?"

In reality...

The man entering the apartment who I thought was the "angry lawyer/co-loft owner" was apparently a "client."

The man building something from the ceiling ... was building, in fact, a swing.

And after years of leasing the loft we discovered there was a random flaw with the intercom system.

Occasionally we could hear who pressed Pamela's intercom and her conversation.

"Now [person so and so] I want you to walk around the block three times."

(We would all then run to the window and look down to see a well-dressed man carrying a single pink Gerber daisy walking around the block in the pouring rain.)

I couldn't help thinking about this business model.

They pay her. She orders them around (or something) and then they do what she orders. (Hmm, "Thank you for the check." "Finish that proofreading—now!")

Jennifer Sterling is a designer, artist, typographer and book designer based in New York. Her work has been exhibited and resides in the permanent collections of the San Francisco Museum of Modern Art, Bibliothèque Nationale de France, Museum für Kunst und Gewerbe Hamburg, the Cooper-Hewitt National Design Museum and the Library of Congress. In 2000, she was inducted into Alliance Graphique Internationale and Who's Who in America. *Graphis* included her in their Top Ten Designers in the World list and *Graphic Design: USA* named her as one of Twelve Designers to Change Design into the Millennium. Additionally she has served on the San Francisco Museum of Modern Art's Design and Accessions Board.

The apartment

by Dana Arnett

Moving is a real world reality that most people inevitably face at some point in their life. And for many, a shift to a new city can be as challenging as it is motivating.

There are the typical hassles that accompany any relocation, but there can also be surprises you would never have dreamed of. Experiences so eye opening, they just may change your life forever.

In 1982, I was about to graduate from Northern Illinois University. Back then, student life on the NIU campus could best be described as a mild mannered, midwestern university experience. This was an average sized state school, made up of average young adults, situated in the most average of communities. Having been raised in a smaller version of DeKalb, I felt very comfortable with the scale and character of this locale. But with graduation just around the corner, I was also ready to move on to something bigger, better and different.

Illinois had record setting weather in May and June of that year. With it came the type of heat and humidity that would make you sweat through your clothes in a matter of seconds. During that eight-week stretch, I was saddled with the task of making weekly apartment hunting trips to Chicago. DeKalb was sixty miles west of the windy city and I had a simple transition plan. I would find an apartment, land a new job, and be settled in just ahead of commencement. It was a good strategy, I thought. A simple plan.

By the fourth week of May, things were quickly turning unpleasant. I had seen over 30 apartments and I was learning the hard way just how complicated it was to find a decent place to rent in Chicago. I essentially had no business (or experience for that matter) navigating the seemingly endless amounts of urban apartment listings. With just a matter of days to go until graduation, I was beginning to have second thoughts about living in Chicago. I was also running out of time.

The day before graduation I turned to my roommate for help. Frank had grown up on the western border of the city, in one of the many "ethnic pockets" that emerged after World War I. Feeling a need to help, he suggested that I might want to stay at his house for a few months until I could find permanent residency. "We have plenty of room," he remarked. "My mom lives there alone and you can move into the upstairs apartment where Granny used to live." "That might be perfect," I remarked. With Granny gone, I could have her entire vacant apartment and move in right away. With a feeling of complete relief and victory, I openly accepted the offer. Frank simply needed to clear things with his mother and we'd be off to the city.

On the Saturday afternoon following graduation, Frank and I loaded up our belongings into a giant U-Haul truck and headed east to Chicago. Free at last. There was nothing more exciting than the promise of a new life and a new career. I hadn't felt this good in a long time, and thanks to the generosity of Frank, my move to Chicago was falling perfectly into place.

We started to reach our destination at about 10:30 P.M. that night. As we pulled into Frank's neighborhood, I was genuinely fascinated with the architecture and character of this vintage Chicago setting. Row-after-row of bungalows dotted the streets—each designed with remarkable similarity, but every one possessing its own unique charm and character. As Frank would explain, these homes were built to serve the immigrant families who moved to the region during the early 20th century. The first floor of a typical Chicago bungalow would serve as the larger living space for young parents and their kids. And the more modest second floor quarters were designed to house the grand parents.

When we finally pulled into Frank's driveway, we were exhausted but filled with a rush of adrenalin. We were finally home, and no matter how tired we were, it was move-in time. We had guessed that his mother had turned in for the evening, but just as we were about to enter, there she stood in full silhouette at the kitchen door. "Who the hell is he?" she remarked as she studied my presence. Frank quickly replied, "This is Dana. Don't you remember we agreed that he would be staying here while he searched for a place in the city?"

....

With that, she grabbed Frank's shirt, pulled him into the house, slammed the door, and proceeded to read him the riot act.

....

I could barely make out the heated exchange as it moved from an intense roar to a muffled shouting match. She obviously had no inkling or interest in the proposed living arrangements, and I was now the apparent centerpiece of a heated family controversy.

About thirty minutes went by and Frank reemerged at the door. We had a conversation on the porch, and I listened reluctantly as he assured me that things were going to be fine with his mother. "She's still a little shook up given all she's been through these last few months." He went on, "With the recent losses of granny and dad, the idea of 'a stranger' living upstairs just hasn't sunk in." "For God sakes, Frank," I said, "you knew of her fragile state and you still allowed this to happen! Are you out of your mind? It's abundantly clear that your mother isn't ready to have a so-called 'stranger' taking up residency under the same roof." Frank calmly reiterated, "Dana, I can assure you that the situation is under control and this is simply a case of my mom overreacting. Tomorrow is a new day and she'll be her old self again. Let's unpack and not get too upset about this. Everything will be fine."

Having finally collected myself, I agreed to set aside the uncomfortable circumstances and move into the apartment upstairs. After all, it wasn't as if I was on the same floor with Frank and his mother. How bad could this be? It was now after midnight and I was ready to call it a day, so decided to set about the task of unloading our belongings.

We started by quietly and conveniently moving Frank's stuff into his old boyhood bedroom. From there, we lugged all of my belongings upstairs to granny's old apartment. Sweaty and exhausted, Frank retired to his bedroom after the last items were moved, and I sat famished, catching my breath, in the front room of my new apartment. I would have to gain a little more strength in order to become settled in. After a few minutes sitting on a pile of boxes, I gathered a second wind and started unpacking a few odds and ends.

The place had a dark and dank feeling as I reached over to flip on the main light switches. After a more thorough look around, I nearly gasped at what I was witnessing. To my left, there was a sink full of dishes covered with aged and crusted foods. To my right, a table was set, not for people, but for eight legged insects that had happily replaced the two former dinner guests. Two plates, one with a half eaten piece of green toast, was the scene of an animated mass of angry grubs. Near the sideboard, cockroaches the size of June bugs milled about the cobwebs in search of their next delicacy. Some clothes and blankets were strewn about couch in front as if they were just placed there. I could go on, but the only words that could begin to describe this site were "crime scene." Apparently, when granny had checked out, so did everyone else.

Pausing in total disbelief, I was trying to reconcile what to do given this incomprehensible situation. This was a true point of reckoning. Should I stay or should I go?

With a sense of perseverance and the determination of Alice from the Brady Bunch, I got to work. In the pantry I found a half-gallon jug of Clorox, a bucket and a mop. With these three tools, I tore into the place. I splashed bleach, scrubbed every surface, and fastidiously cleansed every nook and cranny. I worked with the precision of an undertaker—my cleaning techniques resembling the force of a white tornado. By early dawn, I had completed the remediation process.

It was finally time to turn in so I retired to the bedroom. Barely alert, I slipped into a pair of running shorts and walked over to the bed. With a pull of the covers, I was ready for a long awaited sleep. At that moment, I suppose no sane person could be ready for what I saw next. There laid granny. Well, sort of. It wasn't granny per se, but there, pressed into the muffled mattress, laid a full sized brown imprint of granny's former self. All I could think of was the Shroud of Turin. The body was gone, but the spirit was there in full living color.

As quick as the sheets were pulled, I swept them right back into place with the speed of a jet engine. I may have moved into granny's apartment that night, but I wasn't about to get into bed with her lost spirit. I'd seen a few Wes Craven movies, but living a scene from *A Nightmare on Elm Street* was more than I could take.

Needless to say, my nights thereafter got a whole lot better. I did find a "real apartment" in Chicago, and by all accounts, you could say I was now prepared to face anything and everything. People who hear my story often find it hard time believe, but I can assure you that nothing so vivid could ever emerge from my creative imagination.

As I reflect on this indelible memory, my only advice would be this: Before moving to a new city, bring plenty of disinfectant and make sure granny's still around. There's nothing like the real thing.

Dana Arnett is a founding principal and CEO of the internationally recognized firm of VSA Partners, headquartered in Chicago, with offices in Minneapolis, Detroit and New York City. Arnett, along with his partners, leads a group of 250 associates in the creation of design programs, digital and interactive initiatives and brand marketing solutions for a diverse roster of clients, including: Harley-Davidson, IBM, General Electric, Coca-Cola, Thomson Reuters and Nike.

Over the course of his 28 years in the field, Dana and the firm have been globally recognized by over 60 competitions and designations including; *Communication Arts*, AIGA, *Graphis*, the Type Directors Club, the American and British Art Directors Clubs, *ID*, the LA Film Festival, the AR100 and the American Marketing Association. Arnett was a 1999 inductee into the Alliance Graphique Internationale, and holds the honor of being named to the ID40—who has cited him as one of the 40 most important people shaping design internationally. Arnett is a former member of the AIGA National Board of Directors and he currently serves as a board member of the Architecture and Design Society of the Art Institute of Chicago, and the Chicago Children's Theater. In addition to industry work, Dana is also active as an advisor and member of the business development and venture capital group, Cueball Collective, who help fund and incubate consumer and socially driven ventures.

Cleanest judge in the west

by Eric Rodenbeck

I was nineteen years old, living in New York City, and out of work. I'd been kicked out of Cooper Union the month before (that's a whole other story) and hadn't yet enrolled in the New School, so I was more or less at loose ends.

I was living with five other people in a five-story brownstone in Times Square that we were essentially squatting in (that's another story, too), but even without having to pay rent, I still needed to find a way to make a living. So I started applying for waiter jobs, figuring they'd be easy to get.

Turns out that waiting tables is how everybody and their brother gets their start in New York City, and the competition was much tougher than I imagined it would be. At the end of my fourth failed interview for a waiting job, the bar owner gave me a piece of advice, which showed me how much of a rube (and a grotty teenager) I really was: "If you're going to lie about having previous restaurant experience, you should at least show up for the interview with black pants and clean fingernails. And apply for busboy first, so you learn how to do it." Ouch.

So I took him seriously, bought a pair of black jeans, cleaned up and combed my hair, and went out for my fifth try at Cafe Orlin. I walked down to the interview in the East Village from Times Square, where our house was. Along the way I was approached by a guy who asked to take my picture and get my name. He was a scout for an ad campaign for Levi's jeans, and they were looking for man-on-the-street portraits. I went to the interview, got the job as a busboy and I was on my way.

Photo: Roger Dekker

A few days later I got a phone call, saying that I'd gotten the ad campaign job and could I please show up at this house in the mid-70s on the East Side of Manhattan. The job would pay $1,500. Fifteen hundred dollars! I was a broke busboy in Manhattan and would have chewed my own head off for fifteen hundred dollars. Of course I said yes!

When I got to the house, I met the photographer, a nice older guy named Dick with big black glasses and a mop of white hair. I'd never met him and didn't know much about fashion photography. We talked for a while, he told me what he was going to do, everything seemed fine, so I agreed to the shoot.

His assistants put some goat placenta in my hair (really)—I had never even heard of a placenta before that.

I got into the room and he had a whole setup—pure white paper behind a giant camera, really big, with 8" x 10" negatives mounted on a tripod. He also had two assistants. He started quietly giving orders to his assistants, asking me to move this way and that, and in fifteen minutes we were done.

He gave me a signed copy of a book he'd done, one I'd never heard of. It was called *In The American West*, and the photographer's name was Richard Avedon. Turns out he was one of the most famous photographers in America. He did all kinds of amazing work with *Vogue*, photos in lunatic asylums on Long Island and an incredible set of journeys through the West taking photos of rodeo clowns, cowboys, drunks. All of this was done with his 8" × 10" camera.

Fifteen hundred dollars for fifteen minutes work! It ruined me for life. After that I never wanted an honest job again.

Somehow, I can't quite remember how anymore, I was invited to dinner at his house a couple of days later. In the meantime, we'd had a house party that had gotten out of hand, I'd gotten into a fight with a whole bunch of guys (really!) and had ended up at the hospital. Nothing too major, but I'd been beaten up pretty badly and had a bunch of bandages on my face and on my arm and knuckles.

When I got to dinner at Richard's house, his first words were "We have to do another shoot, promise me you won't touch those bandages in between now and tomorrow!" I did the shoot a couple of days later, and I remember him being very disappointed that I'd taken a shower.

Eric Rodenbeck is the founder and creative director of Stamen, a leading mapping and data visualization design studio based in San Francisco. Recent Stamen projects for the London 2012 Olympics, SFMOMA, MSNBC, MTV, the City of San Francisco, the State of California and others push the boundaries of online cartography and design, while the studio's contribution to open-source mapping projects like Modest Maps, Tile Drawer and Walking Papers are helping enable a bottom-up revolution in how maps and data visualization are made and consumed.

Eric led the interactive storytelling and data-driven narrative effort at Quokka Sports, illustrated and designed at *Wired* magazine and Wired Books, and was a cofounder of the design collective Umwow. He is a sought-after speaker and has lectured and spoken about architecture and data visualizations at Yale University, Harvard, Columbia University, the University of Southern California, numerous O'Reilly technology conferences, Esther Dyson's PC Forum, OFF in Barcelona, Lift in Jeju, Korea, and South by Southwest, among others. His work is in the permanent collection of the Museum of Modern Art in New York City, and he has shown work at galleries and museums in San Francisco, London, Chicago, Minneapolis, Los Angeles and Shanghai.

Eric was born in New York City, where he studied architecture at Cooper Union, put himself through school by managing markets at numerous New York farmers' markets, drafting architectural ornaments in the stoneyard of the Cathedral of St. John the Divine, and working summers for sculptor Kenneth Snelson. He received a B.A. in the History and Philosophy of Technology from The New School for Social Research in 1994. He's been called one of *Esquire* magazine's Best and Brightest new designers and thinkers, and one of *ID* magazine's top 40 designers to watch. He sits on the Board of Directors of the Kenneth Rainin Foundation and the Gray Area Foundation for the Arts, and has been a judge of the National Design Awards sponsored by First Lady Michele Obama.

Magical

by Richard Saul Wurman

In 1958 there was a new pope chosen. He was and older man, chosen as was perceived as a conservative, and accordingly as kind of a "filler" Pope as they weren't worried about him changing policies.

His election came after quite a number of more obviously reform minded Cardinals didn't get the white puff of smoke.

Photo: Melissa Mahoney

He was a homely man, and looked like "the little king" with sort of a spark plug shaped body, but a face that was intriguing and gentle and lovely.

I decided I wanted to see him in person. I obsessed upon this meeting.

I had a trip planned to Europe, a traveling fellowship. It was a rather long trip, 8 months of camping, and I wasn't going to shave the entire time. I told my father that I really wanted to meet this pope, and he mentioned meeting the head of a Catholic charity at an event. The key to this story is that I'm Jewish. My father, a cigar maker, was certainly not in the Catholic Church. But he asked his acquaintance if there was any way I could see the Pope. That man passed along the name of a Monsieur Landi in Rome. I packed up my seersucker drip dry suit and was off.

When I got to Rome, I stayed on the fourth floor of a cheap pensione. I'd written a note to Monsieur Landi, and he'd replied indicating I should come over and see him at his Vatican. So, looking fairly disreputable, I headed off to the Vatican to say hello. The next day, a messenger came over to the pensione with a ticket.

It was extremely hot, as Rome can be in the summer and I got lost. Yes, I know I do guidebooks, but I got lost going there and then couldn't find a place to park. It was jam packed with cars all over.

I finally just left my car in the middle of the road and walked up to this enormous building.

I was late, and sweating, and walked up to the front door and presented my ticket. I was waved in. The place was huge and filled with people. It seemed like there were two thousand people in this auditorium. I never did look up how many people were there, but it was vast.

Further up the center aisle I was sent. I stopped along the way, but then there was someone else that kept waving me up. And they waved me up. And they waved me up onto the stage. There were a couple rows of seats on either side, in a sort of V facing the audience. At the center of the V was a lectern. Everyone in the seats on stage was wearing red. They were Cardinals. I sat down with them, and then the Pope came in.

I was astonished by the Pope. He just seemed to have this mystical aura around him, and the audience clearly loved him. Now, maybe they loved every pope, but it turned out in retrospect that he was particularly the most loved pope in modern history. He spoke many different languages and entranced the audience no matter which he was speaking. When he finished, he did a little blessing to all the cardinals (of course I was there as well), and then he left.

I was moved by this event. In fact, it had an affect on the rest of my life. I realized the joy it is to occasionally be in the presence of extraordinary people. It's not like an adoration of a movie star or sports hero, or one in a position of power. It's just that some people have a centering sense of themselves, of the humor of life itself and the reverence of it at the same time. Yo Yo Ma, Richard Feynman and Lou Kahn all have had it. They're kind of a receiver of, and excreter of, caring, goodness and clarity. I think we call it charisma. There's another mystery out there that has a lot to do with conversation, about people and how they speak with one another. That's the magic I'm talking about and continue to pursue.

. . . .

Spurred by the dance between his curiosity and ignorance, Richard Saul Wurman has sought ways to make the complex clear. He has now written, designed and published 83 books on topics ranging from football to health care to city guides, but he likes to say that they all spring from the same place—his ignorance.

Described by *Fortune* magazine as an "intellectual hedonist with a hummingbird mind," Wurman has been shaped by an epiphany had as a young man: ignorance and embracing the understanding of what it is like to not understand.

Wurman created and chaired the TED conference from 1984 thru 2002 which celebrated his observation of the convergence of the technology business, the entertainment industry and designers. He also created and chaired the TEDMED conference from 1995 to 2010 as well as the eg conferences. Recently, he completed his first www conference and, in 2014, will produce the 555 conference, the first conference to be truly global as it will circumnavigate the globe. "Finding the future first™".

He has been awarded several honorary doctorates, Graham Fellowships, a Guggenheim and numerous grants from the National Endowment for the Arts as well as recently becoming a Distinguished Professor of the Practice of Design in the College of Arts, Media and Design at Northeastern University. He is the recipient of the Lifetime Achievement Award from the Smithsonian, Cooper-Hewitt National Design Awards. Wurman has also been awarded the Annual Gold Medal from Trinity College, Dublin, Ireland, and a Gold Medal from AIGA. He is also a fellow of the AIA and is a board member of The Wolfsonian.

Wurman lives in Newport, RI with his wife, novelist Gloria Nagy, and their three yellow labs, Abraham, Isaac and Jacob.

One rubber glove

by Sean Adams

A few years ago, we decided to make a little self-promo item to send to clients. What everyone needed, we determined, was an emergency kit for unexpected meetings.

Too many times an important client called and asked me to come by immediately after I had reorganized the storage room and was covered in dirt and glue. We bought one thousand little boxes and filled each one with a printed card with meeting tips, a little comb, a pack of gum, mints, the moist towelette packs you get at El Pollo Loco and a button that read "I'm not stupid." This, however, seemed thin, so we decided to add a condom. After all, who knows what might need to be done to secure a job.

Noreen, my business partner, went to Costco to buy the condoms. They come in packs of five hundred there. The next day she returned to the office empty-handed. "I can't do it. It's too embarrassing," she said. So I bought them. Somewhere along the line I thought a better idea was to use the Trojan Magnum extra large condoms. I admit I felt pretty hot when I asked the salesperson if they had packs of 500 Trojan Magnum XL condoms. Everything was fine until I was in line at the cash register. Then I started to feel odd. So I thought it was a good idea to buy some other items to divert attention from my 1500 XL condoms. Unfortunately the only item within reach was the giant container of licorice. It did not occur to me that 1,500 condoms and three containers of licorice looked like someone who liked to lure children into a van.

Later Noreen decided to add one rubber glove to the emergency kit. I don't know why. I don't know what one does with one rubber glove if you aren't a urologist. But I didn't pry into Noreen's private life. I don't want to know.

Sean Adams is a partner at AdamsMorioka. He has been recognized by every major competition and publication including; *Communication Arts, Graphis*, AIGA, the British Art Director's Club, and the New York Art Director's Club. AdamsMorioka has been exhibited often including a solo exhibition at The San Francisco Museum of Modern Art. Adams has been cited as one of the forty most important people shaping design internationally in the ID40, and one of the top ten influential designers by *GDUSA*. In 2013, Sean Adams and Noreen Morioka were the Pacific Design Center Stars of Design awardees in graphic design.

Sean is a past national AIGA president, national board member, and AIGA Los Angeles president. He is a fellow of the Aspen Design Conference, and AIGA fellow. He is a professor at Art Center College of Design. Sean is a frequent lecturer and competition judge internationally. Adams is the author or coauthor of *Logo Design Workbook, Color Design Workbook*, the series Masters of Design, and *Thou Shalt Not Use Comic Sans*. AdamsMorioka's clients include AMPAS, Cedars-Sinai, Disney, Mohawk Fine Papers, the Metropolitan Opera, Natural History Museum, Richard Meier & Partners, Sundance, and the University of Southern California.

How to impress your clients

by Roger Black

We were somewhere near East Quogue when …

Rolling Stone moved to New York in 1977, but I still got to go to San Francisco to work on the new *Outside*, which used our old office on Third Street (until Jann Wenner ran out of money and had to sell the magazine).

Returning from a trip soon after the move, I had to go directly to Montauk for the annual Management Conference, held for about twenty department heads and other key staffers mostly on the business side. The previous year we gathered at Hilton Head, and before that the conference was in Big Sur at the Ventana Inn—but those are other stories. This particular year, Jann showed off his rapid climb up the East Coast by renting a big house out at the end of Long Island and put most of us up at the Montauk Yacht Club.

I came back on the red-eye from SFO, and Annie Leibovitz picked me up at JFK in a black stretch limo. Limos were a regular mode of transportation in those days. (I fondly remember midnight trips to Danceteria and one hysterical ride to Triangle Printing Co. in Philly with Bea Feitler.)

Annie was ready for the trip, if you know what I mean, and by the time we got out to Montauk, we were in a somewhat ripened condition. At the house, the session was raging in full force, led by the advertising department, which was gulping down pina coladas like there was no tomorrow.

A few guests joined the group, for instance John Belushi, who was a regular hanger-out at the new office on Fifth Avenue. The combination of stimulants leaves me with no memory of that evening. First thing the next morning I was to present the redesign of the magazine, featuring a new logo and a more complete installation of our new typeface, both designed by Jim Parkinson. No one was in very good shape, including myself, but at 9:15 A.M. I dragged into the sunroom, where the meeting would take place. Most of the folks had somehow woken up and were finding seats.

I had a screen and projector for the presentation, and I pulled over a bar cart to get the picture to the right height, but the sunroom was hardly dark enough for the slides to show. Fumbling with the French doors, I looked out to the pool and saw Belushi in his bathing suit—a pretty scary thing to see that early in the morning—but it gave me an idea. I reached under the projector and grabbed a bottle of Martel (John's brand), opened the door and waved the bottle at him. Then I closed the door and drew the shades.

Turning to the ragged audience, I said, "Thanks for coming this morning. I appreciate that you showed up so early! I would like to introduce our new associate director, who will be making the presentation."

Everyone blinked at me. Then, with his usual perfect timing, Belushi crashed through the French doors, looking for the cognac.

Everyone applauded. He beamed. He took the bottle, which I had left next to the projector, somehow opened the cork with his thumb and took a swig. I handed him the projector's remote control. He spotted one of those chrome-telescoping pointers in the shirt pocket of Kent Brownride sitting in the front row, and he grabbed it. With a snap of the wrist, *Swot!*, he extended the pointer.

"

Everyone blinked at me. Then, with his usual perfect tim- ing, Belushi crashed through the French doors, looking for the cognac.

"

He pushed the button for the first slide, and we were off.

I'm afraid I don't remember Belushi's exact explanations of the redesign, but it doesn't matter. The audience loved them. Hung-over department heads were roaring, tears streamed down their faces. It was the best redesign presentation I ever made.

After we finished answering questions, one ad salesmen came up to me and said, "That was fantastic. How much did that cost? Can we get him for our next sales meeting?"

For 40 years, working with magazines like *Rolling Stone*, for newspapers like *The New York Times* and web sites like Bloomberg.com, Roger Black has been developing ways to communicate content more effectively. His teams have redesigned *Reader's Digest*, *Esquire*, *Scientific American*, the *Los Angeles Times* and *The Washington Post*.

He is a cofounder of the Font Bureau, and continues to develop new typefaces, and revivals of old ones.

Roger has been working on web sites since 1995 and was involved with some early influential designs, including MSNBC.com and @Home Network. Now he is group creative director of Edipresse Asia and living in Hong Kong.

The Paulgrimage: ghost coyotes in the sand

by Dan Cassaro

You're either a Paul McCartney or you're a John Lennon. Those are your only two options. There are no in-betweens and there are no Ringo Starrs. *All Things Must Pass* is lovely but if you think you're a George Harrison you're just being difficult. There are two sides to this coin/record. One side is "Revolution" and the other is "Hey Jude." Call it in the air.

People who know me know I'm a McCartney. Oh sure, I had a John Lennon phase (coinciding with puberty) and a few George Harrison phases (directly proportionate to the amount of weed I was ingesting), but I always came back to Paul. After stumbling upon Paul's *Ram* in a thrift store many years ago I've developed a special relationship with the record. Sharing it like a secret treasure with loved ones, using it as a litmus test for girlfriends and adopting "Ram On" as my own mantra. Sad and alone? Down on your luck? Doesn't matter. Ram on. It is without any melodrama that I tell you that Paul's songs have carried me through some tough times.

Before I get completely off topic let me switch gears and tell you that this story is about ghost coyotes. Made out of smoke. Dancing in the Mojave Desert at 3 A.M. This Beatles stuff is merely here to help me explain how I got into a very strange situation—the kind of situation in which you might see ghost coyotes. Made of smoke. Dancing in the Mohave Desert at 3 a.m.

Despite being a huge McCartney fan, I had never seen him perform live. I have a very real fear about seeing aging classic rock icons perform in a modern setting. It has the potential to completely ruin the perfect image you have of them in your head. Did you see that Martin Scorsese live documentary about The Rolling Stones? Where Mick Jagger is wear skinny jeans and a pair of weird orthopedic-looking Skechers? Scarring. I didn't want that to happen to me with Sir Paul. But when I heard Paul McCartney was headlining Coachella a few years ago, I felt like I had to go. Coachella is a festival with general admission, so I had just as much chance of seeing Paul up close as anyone else did. The only difference is that I wanted it more. Tickets were purchased, hotels were booked and, because I am an asshole, a white convertible Mustang was rented. The Paulgrimage had begun.

A month later my girlfriend and I were in Indio, California, setting up camp in the front row of the main stage at Coachella. Paul would be on in eight hours. I would be close enough to see the whites of his eyes. The girl next to me had a wings tramp stamp. Everything was perfect.

The next hours tested me. There was no food. We were standing in in direct sunlight. I had very little water. My body felt weak from the heat. Teenagers from Los Angeles inexplicably dressed like sexy

Native Americans surrounded us on all sides. My girlfriend almost passed out. I started to wonder if this may have been a bad decision.

And when things felt like they couldn't get any worse, Morrissey took the stage and reminded me of every terrible girl I dated in my early twenties.

Ram on, I told myself. *Ram on.* After a few wardrobe changes and some songs Morrissey waddled off stage and then, finally, the cruel desert sun set and offered a small amount of relief. Everything was suddenly quiet. When Paul came on all the trials of the past hours— the sunstroke, Morrissey's dumb haircut—seemed to disappear. I don't remember it all clearly, it's mostly just feelings and fireworks. But you know what they say, if you remember seeing a seventy-year-old-Beatle at Coachella, then you weren't really there, man.

On our way back to the hotel I began to come to terms with the fact that eight hours in the hot desert sun with no food or water may have had serious implications on my mental state. Because I was determined to get my money's worth out of the Mustang, the top was down. The vista stretching out in front of me was unsettling. The lines of the unlit two-lane desert highway flashed in my headlights and then disappeared under the belly of the car. With my girlfriend nodding off in the passenger seat and no other signs of life within view there was nothing else to do but stare into the blackness and replay the show in my mind. And that's when they appeared. Just one at first. And then dozens of them. Coyotes. Black coyotes, made of smoke, pouring out into the road in front of me and disappearing in small clouds just as fast. *Ghost coyotes*, I thought. *Nothing to be alarmed about*, I told myself. *You just had a little too much sun today. Don't tell your girlfriend; she'll make you pull over. You'll have water and warm beer and Doritos in your hotel room. Just keep on driving. Ram on. That's what Paul would want.*

....

The studio of Dan Cassaro is a small but scrappy design practice in Brooklyn, New York, with a focus on type, lettering, logo design, and powerful 70s rock and roll. Dan is a native New Yorker and a frequent get-the-hell-out-of-New-York-er. He was named ADC Young Gun in 2011. His works and projects have received accolades from the *New Yorker, Fast Company, The New York Times Magazine, Rolling Stone, The Wall Street Journal, Esquire* and many major design and illustration publications. He also has pets but doesn't feel like it's appropriate to talk about them in a work bio.

A little about my father

by Michael Cronan

This is a story that for years I only knew parts of. It was long after my dad was gone that I was able to connect the dots.

I did not know there was more to the story than the parts I had lived (a young man's hubris). Maybe this story is typical of most dads operating in ways my dad did. I know for myself at times I've set up situations (just small, helpful things) that are still opaque to my sons. But, really, I know my dad's style was unique.

My father was, for a while, a classic Mad Man, only he lived a continent away from Madison Avenue. He produced local television and sold airtime for one of the first TV stations in Sacramento. He was the picture of the early 1950s handsome young businessman in a crisp gray tweed suit, French cuffs and a bow tie. I remember the tweed against my cheek as I hugged his leg, which was the scratchiest surface I can remember.

I learned more stuff about my Dad on the way to his funeral than I knew from spending fifteen years with him. My Uncle Jack, four years older than my Dad, whose name was Jerry, filled me in because he knew my Dad would not have told me these things.

That's not to say that Dad was taciturn or noncommunicative. He was a wonderful user of language. He used it to convey that his education outstripped his years in school. His language was impressive to others as well. I could see it in their eyes. The man had a language gift. Perhaps he just never needed to tell me the things that put the pieces of his life into a finer focus for me. Maybe that is what children need to do on their own; that is, find the context of their parents' lives.

One surprising tidbit I learned about my dad was that for years he shared an apartment with a close buddy who happened to be a

"

The thing was that
his bright blue eyes
did not look like
regular eyes. From
my perspective,
they looked like a
spaceman's eyes.

"

nightclub star on the local transvestite circuit. This was 1943. Think about it. His pal was hetero, not that that was important. They dated beautiful women and often went double dating around town.

Another impressive story my Uncle Jack told me involved my father's eyes: My dad was one of the first young children to undergo a double cataract surgery. Back then, the operation meant enlarging the pupil and cutting onto the iris so the subject could "see around" the obstruction. Still the procedure meant a lifetime of seriously intense eyeglasses. That was okay, because he looked cool in glasses. I've never seen a picture of him with the glasses off, except those taken of him swimming. I learned that he drove a delivery truck for a year during the depression without a license because at the time he was classified as legally blind.

The thing was that his bright blue eyes did not look like regular eyes. From my perspective, they looked like a spaceman's eyes.

This uniqueness wasn't overtly obvious, but once you saw it, it was hard to miss. Mostly women were the first to notice his eyes. As they looked into them, they would tilt their heads slightly and a mild expression of wonder would come over their faces. The total effect contributed to a pleasant, thoughtful and interested appearance that he used effectively in sales, although I never saw an ounce of the cynicism I've see with many salesmen.

One small telling note about his character: Dad used to say, "The best salesmen are the easiest sold." In the day of door-to-door salesmen, we always had three vacuum cleaners. A man would come to the door, Jerry would assure Marge, my mom, that he would kindly send the gentleman on his way. Inevitably the salesman would stay for dinner and the next morning we would put the new appliance along with the others in a hall closet. Mom would be laughing about it with friends on the phone. It has been my experience that he was right on the "salesman easiest sold" issue.

I was effectively out of the house when I was fifteen. It was the 1960s and there wasn't much my parents and I agreed on, either politically, artistically or sartorially. I needed to be gone, in the worst way. Out of the blue, or so I thought so at the time, a close friend of the family, who wore leg braces from polio, asked me to come help him with his house and other caretaker chores in return for room and board. I had enough free time for school and to find a paying job. It was to be a complete boon to my life. When I broached the idea with my Dad, he looked at me for a long time and then smiled, shrugged and said if I kept my grades up and came home at least one Sunday a month, we could try it. He said he would get Mom to agree. I was out of there like a shot and sadly didn't look back often.

Nonetheless, as it turns out, my father was extraordinarily present in my development through those years. I was blind to most of it.

A word about my good fortune on becoming a caretaker: Twenty years later I learned that Dad had introduced the idea of my moving in with him to Fred, the family friend. Fred saw the rightness of it and agreed to keep the discussion between them. Dad had chosen wisely. Fred was an amazing character—divorced, successful, a highly ranked chess player, pretty much a genius-level thinker, and he had a way of successfully making up his own rules on just about everything.

We had serious fun living those rules. Midnight foreign film festivals, weekend drives to Mexico and back, chess marathons, deep discussions on Buddhism were all part of the fare. For a fifteen year old with a special driver's permit I was in a kind of exhaustive bad boy heaven.

Although I saw them once or twice a month for a night or a weekend, this new arrangement effectively cut me off from my younger brother and sister as well as Mom and Dad. And I lost the narrative of their lives, only to hear stories sometimes years after the fact. We had a different relationship from then on.

When I turned sixteen it was time to get a car. I effectively had no money as my paying jobs only took care of clothes, school, food and pot. And I was too proud to ask the parents, as by then I had begun to realize what a churl I'd been from twelve to fourteen years old. One day, an older fellow called me and asked if I wanted to buy his car. A 1939 four-door Dodge with running boards and a mohair interior.

I was not hopeful, as he only wanted fifty dollars for it. I anticipated a stinky rust bucket, but on the upside, fifty bucks was what I could make working Friday and Saturday nights vending cola from a tank on my back at motorcycle races.

When I saw the car I nearly passed out. It was beautiful—green with yellow pinstripes, a perfect body and interior with pod headlights and taillights. One or two years short of a classic and with only 30,000 miles! I was like a made man. The older chap delivered the car to my parents' house and stayed for dinner. It was soon clear that Dad had had a part to play in this transaction. But this was a magnificent gift horse, and I sat dumb and happy. Later when I needed tuition for art school, Dad suggested that I contact the Harrah's Casino, as that family collected classic cars. They offered me what amounted to the tuition plus more. Somehow I was the luckiest young Irishman that had ever been. I did not know then that Dad had grown up with the Harrah's kids, and the old chap who sold me the car was a favorite client from the TV days.

My art school career was wonderful, exciting, crazy. Dad arranged to get me connected to a group of four older Jesuits who shared a big gracious house on Stanyan Street. They invited me to dine with them twice a month, and they drilled me on my schoolwork while we drank splendid wines.

Dad came down to the Bay Area every couple of months, "on business." He would take me to Vanessi's in North Beach and mostly listen. On one of these visits I explained that I wanted to take a leave from college. I remember he winced like he was injured. He listened to my reasons and what I wanted to do. Although it qualified as "street rat crazy" in his mind, he expressed his two fears about the prospect: one he was afraid I would not return to collage, and two, he was afraid he would never see me again.

What was street rat crazy about my plan? Here it is, you decide. I planned to hitchhike with my art school friend, Michael Tucker, from San Francisco to New York, fly to Luxembourg and hitchhike through Europe to somewhere in Italy, fly to Tel Aviv, bus to Jerusalem and present ourselves at Hebrew University, looking for positions as archeological assistants. I have always been mad for ancient history. My first-year art history professor, Cedric Crofts, had thrown gas on the flame.

On the next trip down to visit, at dinner Dad produced a letter of recommendation from the president of my college, casually mentioning that he had lunch with him a week before. It was a letter that would have made Indiana Jones proud. I sounded like an advanced graduate student with special achievements in the First Temple studies.

To this day I do not know what my Dad said or did. There might have been exotic beverages served at lunch.

I simply do not know how he extracted this letter without a trainload of blarney. Nevertheless I presented the letter at Hebrew University, and my friend and I were sent to the Dead Sea where we lived and worked very colorful lives. To this day that experience informs my life.

That was a little about my father. But I'd like to add one tiny story more that occurred to my brother, four years younger. My dad has been gone for twenty years, and this story came to me from my brother only a few years ago.

My brother, Chris, is a tall, handsome blond white guy with big blue eyes. When he was thirteen, Dad had arranged for him to go to summer camp. A friend from his service club had made the offer. My brother was excited and looking forward to camping and making new friends. As they drove into the parking lot where the camp bus had been loading, Chris went from anticipation to confusion to panic. My dad had signed him up for a summer at an all black camp. Chris says that he felt like a little marshmallow in an Oreo package as the bus pulled away. Dad acted oblivious as he waved his tall, handsome marshmallow farewell for the summer. For Chris' part, he admitted that the first few days were a little tough (the only other white guy in camp was a counselor), but soon he was forging lasting friendships with is new campmates. Friendships that would take him through high school and beyond.

My dad was almost blind, but he clearly saw what his kids needed. He taught us by example to value and utilize blindness. Especially in the face of self-doubt, prejudice against others or things that would make us small.

....

Michael Patrick Cronan (June 9, 1951–January 1, 2013) was an American graphic designer, artist and an American Institute of Graphic Arts Fellow based in Berkeley California. He was one of the founders of the San Francisco Bay Area postmodern movement in graphic design that became known as the Pacific Wave, and a recognized corporate identity designer, acknowledged for the naming and the identities of TiVo, Verio, the Indigo, Onyx and Crimson computer lines for Silicon Graphics (SGI) and naming Amazon Kindle.

Contributors

Aaron Draplin
Draplin Design Co.
Portland, OR
draplin.com

Alex Bogusky
Fearless Revolution
fearlessrevolution.com

Alexander Isley
Alexander Isley, Inc.
Redding, CT
alexanderisley.com

Alissa Walker
Gelatobaby
Los Angeles, CA
awalkerinLA.com

Allan Chochinov
New York, NY

Andrew Johnstone
Semi-Permanent
Redfern, Australia
andrewjohnstone.com

Ann Willoughby
Willoughby Design
Kansas City, MO
willoughbydesign.com

Armin Vit
UnderConsideration
Austin, TX
underconsideration.com

Art Chantry
Art Chantry Design
Tacoma, WA

Bonnie Siegler
Eight and a Half
Brooklyn, NY
8point5.com

Brian Singer
Facebook
San Francisco, CA
iamsomeguy.com

Carin Goldberg
Carin Goldberg Design
New York, NY
caringoldberg.com

Charles S. Anderson
Minneapolis, MN
csadesign.com
csaimages.com

Chris Coyier
CodePen
Milwaukee, WI
chriscoyier.net

Chris Heimbuch
Square
San Francisco, CA
squareup.com

Chris Hill
HILL
Houston, TX
hillonline.com

Christian Helms
Helms Workshop
Austin, TX
helmsworkshop.com

Christopher Simmons
MINE™
San Francisco, CA
minesf.com

Dan Cassaro
The Studio of Dan Cassaro
Brooklyn, NY
youngjerks.com

Dana Arnett
VSA Partners
Chicago, IL
vsapartners.com

Debbie Millman
Sterling Brands
New York, NY
debbiemillman.com

DJ Stout
Pentagram Design
Austin, TX
pentagram.com

Dress Code
New York, NY
dresscodeny.com

Eric Baker
Eric Baker Design
Montclair, NJ
ericbakerdesign.com

Eric Rodenbeck
Stamen Design
San Francisco, CA
stamen.com

Erik Spiekermann
EdenSpiekermann
Berlin, Germany
edenspiekermann.com

Gail Anderson
New York, NY
gailycurl.com

Hideki Nakajima
Nakajima Design
Tokyo, Japan
nkjm-d.com

James Victore
James Victore Inc.
Brooklyn, NY
jamesvictore.com

Jeff Greenspan
BuzzFeed
New York, NY
jeffgreenspan.com

Jeffrey Zeldman
Happy Cog™
New York, NY
alistapart.com

Jennifer Morla
Morla Design
San Francisco, CA
morladesign.com

Jennifer Sterling
Jennifer Sterling Design
New York, NY
jennifersterlingdesign.com

Jessica Helfand
WINTERHOUSE
Hamden, CT
winterhouse.com
designobserver.com

Jessica Hische
San Francisco, CA
jessicahische.is/awesome

Ji Lee
Brooklyn, NY

John Maeda
Rhode Island School of Design
Providence, RI
risd.edu

John Sabel
Redondo Beach, CA

Josh Higgins
San Francisco, CA
joshhiggins.com

Lana Rigsby
Rigsby Hull
Houston, TX
rigsbyhull.com

Marc Atlan
Marc Atlan Design, Inc.
Los Angeles, CA
marcatlan.com

Marian Bantjes
Bowen Island, BC, Canada
www.bantjes.com

Matteo Bologna
Mucca Design Corp
New York, NY
mucca.com

Michael Cronan
:: Cronan ::
Berkeley, CA
www.cronan.com

Michael Vanderbyl
Vanderbyl Design
San Francisco, CA
vanderbyldesign.com

Mick Hodgson
Ph.D, A Design Office
Santa Monica, CA
phdla.com

Nancy Skolos
Skolos-Wedell
Canton, MA
skolos-wedell.com

Pamela Williams
Williams and House
Avon, CT
williamsandhouse.com

Randy Hunt
Etsy
Brooklyn, NY
etsy.com
randyjhunt.com

Richard Saul Wurman
Newport, RI
rsw@wurman.com

Richard van der Laken
Designpolitie
Amsterdam, Netherlands
designpolitie.nl

Rick Valicenti
Thirst / 3st
Chicago, IL
3st.com

Roger Black
New York, NY
rogerblack.com

Roman Mars
99% Invisible
Kensington, CA
99percentinvisible.org

Scott Thares
Wink
Minneapolis, MN
wink-mpls.com

Sean Adams
AdamsMorioka
Beverly Hills, CA

Stanley Hainsworth
Tether, Inc.
Seattle, WA
tetherinc.com

Stefan Bucher
344 Design, LLC
Pasadena, CA
344lovesyou.com

Stefan Sagmeister
Sagmeister & Walsh
New York, NY
sagmeisterwalsh.com

Theresa Neil
Theresa Neil Strategy & Design
Austin, TX
theresaneil.com

Vanessa Eckstein
Blok Design
Toronto, Ontario, Canada
blockdesign.com

Vince Frost
Frost Design
Surry Hills, NSW Australia
frostdesign.com.au

Yang Kim
Peopledesign
Grand Rapids, MI
peopledesign.com

Damn Good

By Tim Lapetino and Jason Ada

Damn Good is a unique book that showcases the favorite work of designers from around the world! You'll see the projects they are most passionate and proud of. This diverse collection pushes the boundaries of graphic design, all while chronicling the stories behind the work—in the words of the creative teams who designed them.

Self-Portrait as Your Traitor

By Debbie Millman

Debbie Millman's illustrated essays and visual poems are part philosophy, part art, part deeply personal memoir exposing the universal triumphs and tribulations of being human. Her hand-lettered typography—sometimes tender, sometimes gritty, always breathtaking in its visceral candor—makes *Self Portrait as Your Traitor* a moving masterpiece of a singular art form that speaks to our deepest longings for beauty, honesty, and the ineffable magic of what it means to live.

For more news, tips and articles, follow us at Twitter. com/HOWbrand

For behind-the-scenes information and special offers, become a fan at Facebook. com/HOWmagazine

For visual inspiration, follow us at Pinterest.com/HOWbrand

Find these books and many others at MyDesignShop.com or your local bookstore.